MOSES
on

LEADERSHIP

OR WHY EVERYONE
IS A LEADER

RICHARD KOCH

CAPSTONE

First Published 1999
Capstone Publishing Limited
Oxford Centre for Innovation
Mill Street
Oxford OX2 0JX
United Kingdom
http://www.capstone.co.uk

British Library Cataloguing in Publication Data
A CIP catalogue record for this book is available from the British Library

ISBN 1-900961-60-1

Typeset in 11/15 Bembo by
Sparks Computer Solutions, Oxford
http://www.sparks.co.uk
Printed and bound by
T.J. International Ltd, Padstow, Cornwall

This book is printed on acid-free paper

For Chris and Donna

Contents

Everyone is a Leader

You're probably a leader.

Every executive is a leader or a potential leader. Anyone who has people reporting to her is a leader – maybe a very bad one, but a leader nonetheless. Every supervisor is a leader. Even executives who are apparently lone wolves, who supervise nobody, have influence and therefore need to think of themselves as leaders.

Something like a quarter of all employees in developed countries have leadership responsibilities. That's tens of millions of Americans, Germans and Japanese, tens of millions of French and British people.

But leadership is not confined to work.

Many other people, who are not managers or even not in business, are leaders. All parents are leaders. All volunteers are leaders. All teachers are leaders. All writers and communicators are leaders. Those in politics are leaders.

This is a book for you.

A new source of insight into leadership – religion!

Here are some insights into leadership. The insights have been tested against one of the great stories of leadership – Moses and the Israelites. For those of you unfamiliar with the story, it is explained on page 3. But it is a story of naked leadership, of a man taking his people from disease and oppression through many trials and difficult times to the famed promised land. It is a story whose main events are well documented. It is the ideal test for any theories about leadership.

The Moses story is also much more than a test of ideas about leadership. It helps us see what leadership really is – a process of giving direction and creating followers. It also shows us that leadership is not all that difficult: you don't have to have a great intellect; you don't have to be tall; and you don't need a magnetic personality. You have to know where you are headed; you have to have some beliefs and values that will be attractive to your followers; and you have to have good timing. With these ingredients, you can be a great leader. The task you face is not simple, but it is not calculus. You need to take your sense of direction, your beliefs and values and your judgement and do three things.

1   Start with a cause

To lead well, you must excite.

Good leaders turn people on. A tiny minority of leaders do this by what most of us think of as inspiring leadership: by charisma, force of personality, unusual charm or compelling presence. You either have this or you don't, and most of us don't. If leadership required charisma, the world would be a much poorer place.

It doesn't require exceptional interpersonal skill to excite people. It requires a Cause: something that gets people to want change to happen.

Freedom is a great Cause. *Eliminate starvation* is a great Cause. *Build a cathedral* is a great Cause. A Cause is attractive to those you want to influence. Good Causes are often about moving away from something as much as they are about moving towards something. Freedom *from* (persecution, slavery, starvation) more than freedom *to* (do what you like, own a house, work 35 hours a week). In business, 'safety' can be a good Cause, as can 'quality', especially when these causes are safety *from* injury and quality *rather than* shoddy work.

You cannot become an effective leader without a Cause. You cannot contribute to progress without a Cause. You cannot do good or ill without a Cause. Without a Cause, you leave little imprint on the world.

A Cause mobilises. A Cause attracts. A Cause that you can persuade others to get excited about is the beginning.

2   *Found a religion*

A Cause gives you direction and it gives you some early followers. A Cause positions you on the first rung of leadership. The next rung is to convert your early followers into disciples. This requires creating a religion.

We are not talking here about a cult – a fanatical group of people driven forward by a weird set of beliefs. But we are talking about the secular equivalent. The equivalent of a cult in business terms, in family terms or in organisation terms. A successful leader creates a group of followers who are determined, committed in their beliefs and self-confident about what they are trying to do. It's a form of cult: a clan, band or tightly knit organisation. In the terms of this book, it's a religion.

Most business people do not realise the force of religious zeal. If you are going to lead people in a way that turns them on, you need to give them a sense of purpose, and bind them into a winning team with its own distinct ways of doing things. The organisations best at doing this are religions: always have been. Religions create that sense of common purpose that energises people.

There is a tendency today to think that business is a process to be engineered or re-engineered, downsized or upsized; a set of economic transactions, defined by customers, suppliers and competitors; a quest for nothing more (nor less) than constantly compounded profits and market values. Of course, business *is* all of these things. But successful business is an expansionary crusade, or it is nothing. Every successful business is an expansive religion. It is constantly gaining converts, both as co-operators (employees, suppliers, distributors) and as customers.

You can run a successful business, department, school, voluntary activity, political party or home without a religion or without realising you have a religion. But you cannot *lead* it well without one.

Creating a religion is about understanding your followers, making sure they have many shared experiences (successes and failures), and helping them to develop some shared beliefs and values. It's a gradual process, not a one-time evangelical experience. It needs to be worked on over months not days, or years not months – it depends on the size of your ambitions. If you want your followers to be pursuing the cause in 1000 years' time, you need to spend two or three generations developing the religion. If you want to complete your cause by Friday week, you need only spend two or three days developing your religion.

3   *Leaders have good timing*

Good leaders are like good musicians, good actors, good comedians. Their timing is impeccable.

You can have the best ideas, the best product, the best procedures, the best followers, the best organisations, the best contacts. But if you don't have good timing, your leadership will be fatally flawed.

Timing is an art. But like most art, timing can be observed, learned, practised, and, if not always perfected, it can always be greatly improved.

There are three steps where timing is vital: when to launch your Cause, when to codify your religion and when to step down as leader. Get these wrong and your efforts as a leader will be stillborn because you have no fellow travellers; face an early death because you lose your followers; or destroy what you have created because your followers rise up against you.

A Cause should be launched when there is unrest. The followers you want must be unhappy. They must have tried a few early solutions and failed to solve their problems. They must be angry more than weary, frustrated more than fatalistic, and revengeful more than wounded. You need to sense this dissatisfaction and hurt pride. You need to tap into this energy.

As you work together, live together, or do whatever it is you are doing with your followers, they will start growing together. It won't be a smooth process, but it will happen. There will be fights and factions, passionate relationships and poisonous relationships, hatred and happiness. Your role is to ease tensions, develop working practices, set precedents, keep the gradual bonding process moving forward. But this is not enough – at some point you have to lead by nailing your colours to the mast, by making it clear what you believe in and what you do not believe in – what your religion is about.

The timing of this codification is crucial. You must have waited long enough to be confident of majority support. Your disciples will have been pushing you to come clean for some time. But you will have waited until you are confident of the majority. You will also not have waited too long. Rival factions will have been gaining strength and you need to declare your hand before they are too well entrenched. Once you have codified your religion you have to live by it – walk the talk. You need to wait until you know you are strong enough to discipline those who don't. Timing is all.

Finally, you should time your exit. Good leaders are remembered as such because they don't outstay their welcome. A remarkable proportion of those we think of as great leaders – from Alexander the Great to Jesus Christ to John F. Kennedy – had the good fortune to die young. Their lives were cruelly cut short but their reputations mercifully extended. Many terrific leaders spoiled great performances by hanging on too long: look at Queen Victoria, J. Edgar Hoover, Margaret Thatcher, Pope John Paul II. At a less exalted level, compare John Lennon with Frank Sinatra, Elvis Presley with Cliff Richard.

When your Cause is no longer fresh, when the religion starts to ossify, when the expansion slows down, it's time to hand over to a new leader.

Leadership as a journey

We can learn a lot about leadership from the epic journeys of myth and literature, and from the way that successful religions have been formed. The story of Moses combines both strands: epic journey and successful new religion. We therefore follow the story of Moses from start to finish, to see how he launched his leadership bid and founded an amazingly durable religion – using the story to discern a clear pattern of successful leadership.

These journeys all start out with certain ideals and intentions, but with uncertainty about the exact direction or how to get to the goal. Gradually, the map unfolds and the goal becomes more definite and attainable, but not before some dramatic reversals of fortune. The journeys involve tests of character and calculation, courage and cunning. There are always opposing forces of evil, who win their fair share of battles before losing the war. There are usually traitors and false prophets, as well as allies and supporters.

Epic journeys convey much of the flavour of the modern corporate quest for 'purpose' at work. They are a useful corrective to the seductive, prevalent view that progress in corporate change management can be linear, straightforward, logical, planned from the outset and inevitably successful. Most modern management writers seem bizarrely unaware of the dimensions of power, ambiguity, frustration and conflict that make corporate life fascinating to observe and challenging to negotiate.

In choosing one epic journey to illustrate the tools, I considered a number which do have strong parallels, including the works of Homer and Bunyan. In the end, however, I came to realise that *all* the insights could be derived from an even older story: that of Moses leading the people of Israel out of slavery in Egypt, across the Red Sea, around the wilderness, on to Mount Sinai to receive the Ten Commandments, and then on to the final journey to the Promised Land. Many readers will be old enough to recall the marvellous film *The Ten Commandments* starring Charlton Heston, replete with Cecil B. de Mille miracles and fireworks. Some readers will also recall the story directly from the *Old Testament*. But do not be put off if the story is unfamiliar. The insights the story provides about how to give purpose to a people are plain enough. The parallels do not need to be forced.

Your own leadership journey

Think about your leadership task as a journey. If you're the leader of a group of scouts, a class of students, the canteen, the photocopying department, or General Motors, what is your journey going to be? Where are you heading and why? When will you start out? Or have you already started? Do you have followers? Where are you on the journey? Have you formed a religion yet? Have you codified it? Do you have disciplines? Are you on the road to the promised land? Have you arrived? Are you thinking of standing down?

Leadership vignettes

Throughout the book we lob in boxed vignettes of good and bad leadership. Many, but if not all, of these are business examples. Executives should find many parallels with their own organisations. We hope that other leaders will also find insight relevant to their own teams too.

The examples show more or less effective leadership, not good or bad leaders. Leadership depends more on the situation and timing than on the inherent attributes of the leaders.

There *is* skill in leadership – it's not all a matter of luck. But leadership skill can be learnt. You can always be a much better leader – and so too can everyone else. Pay attention! You have nothing to fear but failure to learn.

Part 1

The Moses Tour

Part One tracks the epic journey of Moses – a story of liberation, anguish, revolt, boredom, ecstasy, and of the gradual development of one of the world's great nations and religions. The story is both dramatic and simple, but above all – why else would we be interested in it? – it is a great demonstration of leadership in action. At each stage of Moses' odyssey we can get clear and unusual insights into how to lead: how to exert positive influence to achieve what we want.

It is a bit difficult to believe that modern people, of all religions and none, can get in the driving seat by reviewing an ancient Hebrew tale. Yet it is so. Follow the story and you will know how to become a really effective leader.

Chapter 1 summarizes the story and its five steps to effective leadership. Each of the following five chapters covers one of the steps, following the sequence of the Moses tour.

Are you sitting comfortably? Then let's begin ...

Five Steps to the Promised Land

Consider the story in outline. A senior Egyptian, Moses, is aware that his people are enslaved. He decides to liberate them by stealth. He uses a run of bad luck for the Egyptian economy and environment – the plagues – to negotiate with the President for the release of his tribe (the first recorded management buy-out proposal). The President agrees to the deal, but then reneges.

Moses decides to go ahead anyway, and organises a freedom march for his 600,000 people. The authorities rather belatedly discover this exodus, and give chase. Moses' people, the tribe of Israel, are trapped between the advancing Egyptian army – with their new-fangled chariots – and the Red Sea. At the last minute, Moses gives the order to advance into the sea – and apparent sudden death. A freak storm causes the waters to rise in two places so as to allow the tribe to walk across the Sea on dry land. The Egyptians pursue, but as Moses escorts the last of the tribe on to the opposite bank, the wind drops and the sea rushes back, engulfing the pursuing Egyptian army and sinking it without trace.

Having crossed the Red Sea, the tribe tries to find its way in the wilderness, but finds the terrain tough and uninviting. Supplies run short. There is no food in the desert. Moses faces a revolt. A pro-Egyptian party springs up to urge a retreat to Egypt, on the not unreasonable grounds that slavery is better than starvation. Moses solves the problem by securing daily deliveries of 'manna from heaven' (a mysterious substance able to provide both physical and spiritual nourishment). His opinion poll rating starts to recover. Moses then uses the time in the Sinai desert to organise his tribe into smaller units under a series of leaders and subleaders. He also develops the culture of the tribe, with a series of rituals which gradually erode adherence to the old religion. Dissidents are rooted out, encouraged to return to Egypt, or converted to the new religion.

Some years on, Moses climbs Mount Sinai to receive inspiration and to decide where to lead his people. He comes down from the mountain with new conviction and a set of rules of behaviour for his people – the Ten Commandments. He then vigorously purges the remaining pockets of resistance to his new religion. The visit to Mount Sinai defined his religion once and for all.

There follows the final journey to the Promised Land. The people know where they are heading and can see the rewards ahead in the land of milk and honey. But the land is occupied by a competing tribe that is highly regarded. The people of Israel begin to lose heart again. Another pro-Egyptian party gains ground. Gradually, however, Moses and his followers gain the upper hand, the battle for the hearts and souls of the tribe. A few signal victories over competitors en route gives the people self-confidence and dedication to the cause. In the end, the people march victoriously into the Promised Land, although Moses himself dies before this happens, and a new generation of leaders takes over.

The individual stages of the journey are discussed in more detail below and in Chapters 2–6. But as you read and reflect on the journey, keep on the lookout for three recurrent 'change management' themes:

- *The difficulty in changing culture.* Old habits do die hard. It was easier to get the tribe out of Egypt than to get Egypt out of the tribe.
- *The time it takes to effect lasting change.* Change can be planned rather than left to chance, but patience and perseverance are the price of lasting impact.
- *The need for new behaviour standards to fit a new purpose.* Change is only successful when people in the team start behaving differently. This requires conscious manipulation and gradual adaptation.

Now, on to each of the Five Steps.

Step one: crossing the Red Sea

For the leaders, this is all about summoning up the will to change things. About deciding to leave the security of the status quo. Being willing to set out on a long journey with only team spirit and a cause.

You can't cross the Red Sea until you have rounded up your band of followers. Decide who is going to be in your team. This may be the existing team *in toto*, the existing team with a few people dropped and added, or a completely new team. Select your team with care. It must be a team that you will enjoy working with, and that will find your Cause as appealing as you do.

Next, you need a Cause. This is the banner the team will hoist at the start. What the team stands for. The Cause must be an improvement on the status quo. The Cause is the immediate reason for the journey. Remember that tough times may lie ahead. At the start it is exciting. But when you are hungry and in the desert, you are going to need to know why you put yourself in this mess.

Many would-be travellers to the Promised Land never get round to setting out. But if and when you do, miracles can start to happen.

For the facilitators, this step is about galvanising the leaders to act, perhaps pushing them into it: leading from behind. At the very least, make sure that you are close behind the leaders, or you risk being drowned or left behind in Egypt.

Step two: forming a tribe

For both leaders and followers, crossing the Red Sea was exciting and once the leaders had made up their minds it didn't take long. Now comes the first difficult bit, which can also be tedious. In the original version of events there was a rather long wait trudging round the wilderness, building up a proper tribe, working out the lie of land and what was special about the Chosen People. You must now go through a similar process, even if it doesn't take a full 40 years.

For leaders, forming a tribe means getting to know your people, appreciating your team's unique history and culture, and beginning to develop or celebrate some shared values. It also means doing your homework on your own people, their needs and aspirations, and undertaking reconnaissance on your surroundings. For business teams, you need to know the wishes of customers, suppliers and the local community, as well as those of your employees. Who are you fighting against, and is your strategy against competitors working? Do your values fit the needs of your company in strategic terms, and does the strategy help to reinforce the values you want? For other organisations, you need to understand all those involved with or being influenced by your activity (your stakeholders) and think about other groups who are competing with you for the attention of stakeholders.

The key thing in building a religion is *your team's contribution to others*. The team should have fun, but your party should not be the same as everyone else's party. The difference can only reside in the difference you make to other people's lives and the way that you do it. Your religion must be different and benevolent. Otherwise, why should it expand?

Forming a tribe means sketching out the religion in outline, and beginning to explore your unique destiny. It's a tricky step, but indispensable.

For followers, this is the most dangerous part of the journey. Don't lose heart if you seem to be going round in ever-decreasing circles – this is par for the course, and though your leaders don't really yet know whether they are going, you'll all get there eventually. It will take time. Be faithful to the cause you all started out with, and don't for heaven's sake try to depose your leader or go whoring off after false gods, or there'll be no end of trouble. Lay in large supplies of mineral water and be patient.

Step three: the visit to Mount Sinai

For everyone, this is even more exciting and spooky than crossing the Red Sea. The high point of the process.

The time has come when *leaders* must codify the religion. You will be under pressure to continue backing two or more religions, but you must now choose. Your leaders will declare the Ten Commandments telling you and your people how to behave in the future.

For facilitators, if the leaders spend more than a month up on Mount Sinai, send out a search party. Take some strong sunglasses. When the leaders do return, observe what top management does as well as what they say. But realise that team behaviour standards have now been cast in stone, and don't be the first to be punished for contravention of the new rules.

Step four: journey to the Promised Land

The whole tribe can see the Promised Land from Mount Sinai, but it's still quite a long way off, and getting the whole organisation there is a major logistical exercise.

Leaders must discover how to make the religion work with all your people. You need to go amongst them and explain what future they must create. You need to preach the Ten Commandments, and elaborate them into a detailed guide for behaviour.

The religion is still very young and fragile. You need to ensure it has its devoted missionaries to kindle enthusiasm, its priests to spot and excoriate backsliding, and its monks to refine the religion and take it to higher standards. It may also help to burn a few unrepentant heretics at the stake, *pour encourager les autres*.

For facilitators, you are entitled to see yourselves as founder members (lay priests) of the new religion. For other *followers*, convert early to it. This will make you feel more fulfilled, and also do no end of good to your career.

Step five: arriving in the Promised Land

Everyone will know when the tribe has arrived. You won't be greeted with a twenty-foot sign on the outskirts saying that, 'Heaven Welcomes Careful Pilgrims'. But the milk and honey will be thick on the ground. The religion will seem natural and an eternal tradition, rather than a recent invention.

Now is the time for *leaders* to stand back and see if the religion is good, if there are pockets of continued resistance, and if the task has been fully accomplished. It should now be an irreversible process, so that even if the whole top team went down in a 747, the new religion would still be secure.

To avoid arrogance or complacency, leaders should already be thinking about the adaptations to the religion necessary in the next decade. And this would also be a good time to hand on to a new generation of leaders. As Moses realised, this is the best way to bequeath a living legacy and keep your reputation at its zenith.

The whole tribe will enjoy a new sense of purpose and contribution. What the team does will be fun and important.

Back down to earth

You've just had an eagle's eye view of the process, without telling you how you actually jump the hurdles. If the journey still appeals, now is the time to come down to earth and provide you with the Official Exodus Route Map.

A new religion at BP – how to lead and be ousted

'Batman shakes BP to bedrock' gushed *Fortune* magazine six months after Bob Horton became chairman of British Petroleum, the fourth largest free market oil company in the world. Horton had earned the nickname 'Batman' as a result of his whirlwind revitalisation of BP's largest subsidiary, Standard Oil of Ohio. He had worked closely with a financial adviser, John Browne, and, as they swept through Standard Oil cutting back, restructuring and revitalising, the two became known as Batman and Robin – Horton being big and burly, Browne small and quick.

In March 1990 Horton was appointed chairman of BP. Over the previous six months he had prepared himself for the moment. So when he took the reins, he announced wide-ranging cultural and organisation changes. He announced a total shake up of BP.

His culture change programme, supported by many consultants and change gurus, was highly visible. He invited the *Financial Times* to be a fly on the wall. Articles began to appear in journals and magazines, and BP managers spoke about change management at external conferences. Horton was clearly committed. The *Financial Times* referred to it as a corporate metamorphosis.

The problem, as reported in *Fortune*, was BP's bureaucratic culture. The company had spent much of its history as a government department and had acquired the attitudes and working methods of the British civil service. As Horton explained, 'When I returned from Cleveland to London, I spent six months in deep culture shock because, until I had been away for a couple of years, I hadn't realised how deeply embedded the bureaucracy, the distrust, the second-guessing had become. We want to move to a more flexible organisation that works on trust and openness and teamwork.' It was clear that Horton was trying to wake up and shake up his company.

As observers of this drama, we were fascinated to find out whether Horton was tackling the task of waking up BP in the way we believe is appropriate. We wanted to know whether Horton was taking the right path to the promised land. At the end of each of the following chapters, we will refer back to Bob Horton's experience and give him some advice. We will tell you what we would have said to Horton if we had been his advisers. We will draw out the essence of each chapter and use it to advise 'Batman'.

But first we should tell you what happened at BP, and to do this we have to go back to the period before Horton was appointed. Six months

Fig. 1 BP's central organisation

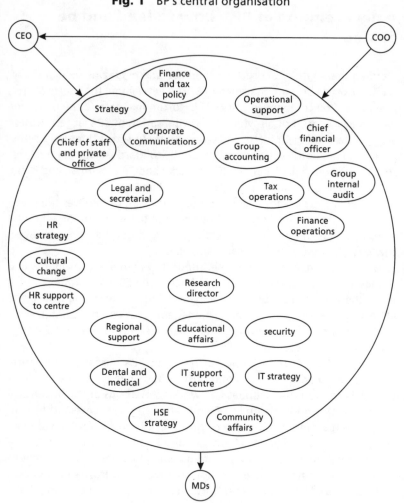

before he was appointed, Horton put together a project team of young, energetic managers to take a fresh look at BP, 'unconstrained by the outcome of previous studies and without any blueprint for change'. The project became known as PROJECT 1990, and the remit was:

- To reduce complexity throughout the corporation
- To re-design the central organisation
- To reposition the corporation in approach and style for the 1990s.

PROJECT 1990 proposed some radical solutions. One thousand one hundred and fifty posts were eliminated at the corporate centre, 80 standing committees were abolished, 11 managerial layers were collapsed into 6, a teamwork-oriented structure was developed for the central organisation (refer to Fig. 1) and a new vision and values statement was launched with the purpose of 'becoming the most successful company in our field, the best to work for, buy from and do business with.' It was clear that Horton intended to make changes across a broad front.

To support these changes implementation teams were put together. The Culture Change Team arranged workshops and seminars for 'the top 230' managers, hired outside speakers, developed behaviour guidelines, launched task forces on career development, performance appraisal, etc., and carried out many other initiatives. BP, particularly at the centre, was turned upside down. Every single person working at the centre had taken part in one of the workshops by early 1991.

Much of the effort was devoted to practical issues of the new organisation. But time was also devoted to discussing a vision and values statement and the growing jargon of 'empowerment', 'networking', 'team work', 'open thinking', 'personal impact', etc. A new language was growing up with the new philosophy and managers needed to understand what it all meant. The *Financial Times* estimated that BP probably spent £20 million on its change programme in the first two years.

It was clear that all this change could not be achieved without pain, and during 1991, journalistic pieces appeared suggesting that all was not well at BP. Strategically the company was under tremendous pressure because of high borrowing and a low oil price. Moreover, BP's success was built around two oil fields that were maturing fast. Horton announced more cutbacks and lay-offs.

By February 1992 the odd critical article had become a torrent of concern about BP's future, often quoting disenchanted insiders. Poor results, an unfortunate gaffe in an interview that revealed Horton's natural and self-assured arrogance, and a clear disagreement in the Board about the appropriate dividend policy led to Horton's surprise resignation. The reason – policy differences and his forceful, if not abrasive, management style.

David Simon, his replacement, was at pains to point out that the strategy and the culture change programme would continue as before, that the change in leadership was more about style than about strategy. Yet the *Economist*, in a focus on BP, commented 'since ousting its boss in a boardroom coup, BP has insisted it will not change course. This could be a big mistake, for almost every aspect of the company's strategy has gone awry.'

It is clear that the cultural revolution initiated by Horton was not abandoned. Horton will be remembered as someone who shook up BP, but he will not be remembered as the founder of a 'new BP'. He was not given the chance to complete the job, even if he was capable of doing so.

Chapter 2

Oops! Getting Through the Red Sea

The people of Israel journeyed from Rameses to Succoth, about 600,000 men on foot, besides women and children ... and very many cattle ... When the king of Egypt was told that the people had fled, the mind of Pharaoh and his servants was changed, and they said, 'What is this we have done, that we have let Israel go from serving us?' So he made ready his chariot and took his army with him ... and he pursued the people of Israel as they went forth defiantly ... When Pharaoh drew near, and the people of Israel lifted up their eyes, and behold, the Egyptians were marching after them; and they were in great fear. And the people of Israel cried out to the Lord; and they said to Moses, 'Is it because there are no graves in Egypt that you have taken us away to die in the wilderness? For it would have been better for us to serve the Egyptians than to die here.'

And Moses said to the people, 'Fear not, stand firm, and see the salvation of the Lord; for the Egyptians whom you see today, you will never see again. The Lord will fight for you, and you have only to be still.'

... Then Moses stretched out his hand over the sea; and the Lord drove the sea back by a strong east wind all night, and made the sea dry land, and the waters were divided. And the people of Israel went into the midst of the sea on dry ground, the waters being a wall to them on their right hand and on their left. The Egyptians pursued, and went in after them into the midst of the sea, all Pharoah's horses, his chariots, and his horsemen ...

Moses stretched forth his hand over the sea, and the sea returned to its wonted flow ... and the Egyptians fled into it, and the Lord routed the

Egyptians in the midst of the sea … But the people of Israel walked on dry ground through the sea …

Thus the Lord saved Israel … and Israel saw the Egyptians dead upon the seashore … and the people believed in the Lord and in his servant Moses.

(From *Exodus*, Chapters 12 and 14.)

How do you get started?

The first hurdle is to work out whether you seriously want to lead, and to get together a very small nucleus (perhaps only one other person, more likely two to four) who are committed to doing this.

Before you decide, and at the risk of seeming timid, may we point out the enormity of the task ahead of you. You are setting out to give a purpose and new energy to your team. So who do you think you are? Moses? You might say, no, of course not, but in a way you are.

You are about to found a religion, something that will be with your team for the rest of its existence. Moses may have a few centuries on you and his people turned out to be more numerous and influential than you are likely to prove, but on a small scale it's the same task.

We're perfectly serious about this. Let's spell it out. You have to decide to leave the warm womb of the status quo behind. You have to find people to follow you, voluntarily and heart and soul, not because you are the leader. You have to be prepared to fight off the status quo 'Egyptians'. You have to found a tribe. You have to discover a Cause for your team that goes beyond the selfish interests of the participants. You have to fashion their values to reflect and underpin the purpose, and draw up the Ten Commandments so that behaviour standards are crystal clear and aligned with the purpose and values. Then you have to spread the gospel, send out missionaries, root out heretics and reward the faithful, so that when you leave your legacy will still stand.

Think before you jump in!

So perhaps you agree: it's a tall order, and if you are one of the top five in your organisation it's an extremely serious step. Do you really want to bite this off? The risk of failure is high. This may be the biggest and toughest decision you will make in your career. Take time over it. Don't be afraid of backing away from it if the conditions are not right or you do not want to take the risk. Once you have crossed the Red Sea there is no turning back and you have to see it through. Many people don't stop to think before they strip off and wade in. To help you avoid this error we have devised the Leaders' Checklist (see below) to see whether you are ready. You should consider four points:

- is there a 'cause' you can see already: a crusade in the making?
- are your followers behind (or even better, ahead of) you?
- can the tribe swim?
- can you deal with political foes?

Is there a Cause?

Before you cross the Red Sea, you need at least a sketchy definition of your Cause: you need to know your God. Moses knew that his God was Yahweh and his cause was the liberation of the Israeli people. He had received a sign that the time was ripe. If you are to cross the Red Sea you need to know in outline what you will be fighting for. Before General Franco landed in Spain from North Africa and raised his standard of revolt against the Republic, he had a cause: maintenance of the Spanish Empire. Before Gladstone decided to wrest back the leadership of the British Liberal Party in 1878, he defined a cause – the liberation of the Balkan peoples from the Turks.

So what is your 'cause'? Your cause will come from you. Something you feel deeply about. It will have links to your upbringing, your values, your religion. It may be something you are afraid of letting out of its box because you are uncertain just how strongly you feel. It could be about the impor-tance of people and empowerment. It could be about a new invention that you believe will be of great value. It is likely to be about behaviour. It is

The Red Sea Checklist

Before embarking on the Red Sea Crossing, check if swimming conditions are safe:

1 Are you seriously prepared to risk your career to do this?
  (a) Yes.
  (b) Perhaps.
  (c) No.

2 Can you define a cause?
  (a) Yes.
  (b) Not quite yet.
  (c) No.

3 Are your followers:
  (a) ahead of you?
  (b) close behind you?
  (c) wandering about willy nilly?

4 Are the new ideas you have:
  (a) clearly workable?
  (b) totally unproven?
  (c) somewhere in between?

5 Is there:
  (a) no serious opposition to your group?
  (b) opposition, but which you know how to neutralise?
  (c) opposition that could unseat you?

6 Do you have reliable co-conspirators:
  (a) Yes.
  (b) Maybe.
  (c) None who can be relied upon.

7 Do you personally have high loyalty to the existing organisation or
  would you consider leading a break-away faction for your cause?
  (a) Very high loyalty, would not consider defection.
  (b) Loyal, but would consider break-away.
  (c) Disaffected, would relish break-away.

Scoring

Q1 and Q2: for each (a) 40; (b) 5; (c) 0.
Q3 and Q5: for each (a) 30; (b) 25; (c) 0.
Question 4: (a) 20; (b) 0; (c) 10.
Q6 and Q7: for each (a) 20; (b) 5; (c) 0.

Results

160–200 points Cross the Red Sea: go for it.
120–155 points Lead a spin off team.
Up to 115 points Stay put or wait for a more opportune time.

likely to be about making a contribution – doing good. But remember if it is too personal you may be entering the Red Sea on your own. It must be a cause others can feel strongly about too. Freedom is a great cause. Efficiency is less easy to win people to. Caring for people is a good cause and eliminating waste is another popular cause. At this stage it doesn't need to be better defined than any of these.

But you must not have multiple causes. You need one clear cause. One brightly coloured flag for your people to follow. One song that everyone can sing. You are going to live with this cause until you visit Mount Sinai so think carefully about it.

The cause must energise you and your followers to cross the Red Sea and sustain you through the difficulties you will face in the desert beyond.

Are your followers pushing you in?

Ideally, the leader should be responding to a ground swell from his or her followers. He shouldn't consider jumping in until the followers are massed behind him on the banks of the Red Sea, and almost forcing him to jump. To continue the two examples above, Franco was virtually the last general to burn his boats with the Republic and he was pushed into revolt by his followers. Gladstone tapped and fanned a wave of righteous indignation which already existed in British public opinion over atrocities committed by the

Filofax: a study in crossing the Red Sea

In the Spring of 1990, David Collischon, Chairman and majority share-holder of Filofax, the personal organiser company, was a worried man. The seemingly inexorable rise of Filofax sales, which had soared in the early and mid-1980s, had come to an end with the 1980s and since then the firm's monthly moving average sales went down, down and down. The media had no doubt that this was associated with the death of the Yuppie.

David had attempted to diversify away from dependence on Filofax's one (apparently dying) product, but without success. He had hired a new managing director with a marketing background, but an expensive advertising campaign had failed to halt the month-by-month sales decline. The company was running out of cash fast.

The parallel with the Exodus story is quite close. Under a different Egyptian regime (in the time of Joseph), the people of Israel had prospered and wielded considerable political clout. Now, in Moses' day, they were slaves. Filofax had experienced an equally dramatic fall from grace. Something needed to be done: but in both cases, no one knew what.

Collischon commissioned a strategy study, which threw up some surprising results. First, the problem was not a market collapse, but loss of market share to cheaper competitors. Second, retailers still believed the Filofax brand was sufficiently strong, with the right products, to command a 15 per cent price premium. Third, overseas markets for personal organisers were growing fast. And fourth, Filofax's costs were far higher than those of competitors, but a combination of overhead slashing and overseas product sourcing could reduce costs to below those of competitors.

Armed with these results, David raised fresh equity capital and started anew. His cause was regaining leadership in the ring binder organiser market.

Now, David Collischon believed again in Filofax's future. So he took a deep breath, and changed the key managers, including the chief executive.

He then took the new team across the Red Sea to follow a cause of regaining leadership. The new team preached the gospel of the personal organiser, abandoned diversification efforts, produced attractive new products, and went single-mindedly into battle to win back market share. A cultural revolution swept through Filofax, based on renewed faith in the brand and the gospel of hard work and team work.

> By the end of 1992, the new approach was clearly working. Moving average annual sales were 40 per cent above their recent low, and still firmly trending upwards. The cash position had turned around, so that Filofax was able to buy Lefax, its one upmarket competitor. Costs had been slashed, gross margins raised, and the share price had more than quintupled in less than two years. A tribe has started to reform at Filofax and soon the company will be ready for a trip to Mount Sinai.

Turks on the Armenians. In 1917 Lenin seized power by exploiting urban unrest which had already become endemic throughout Russia.

In retrospect, leaders often seem to have created their own causes, but the truth is usually the opposite. Successful leaders mobilise a movement that is already there. If there is no such latent crusade, even the most charismatic of leaders will be left high and dry. If there is a cause that will bring the people out, the most unlikely leader can succeed.

Next, consider how able the people are to carry this through …

Can the tribe swim?

The health of the team and its capability to carry through major change need to be considered together.

If the team is fit and flexible, this is a good springboard for change.

Yet, a very successful team may be more difficult to shift than a reasonably successful one. Complacency or euphoria may abound when the team is going from strength to strength and, unless there is some discontent and unease within the company, the status quo may be immovable.

On the other hand, a team that has major unresolved issues, and a deteriorating financial performance, is probably in the worst position for crossing the Red Sea. Until the strategy is sorted out and the tribe is reasonably self-confident about its ability to march forward, crossing the Red Sea is likely to lead to confusion and death in the wilderness.

The other good spring board for change is a crisis. A fight for survival is a great opportunity to build from the bottom. The risks are high. But so is the commitment. Survival is a great cause for launching into the Red Sea.

Most teams that have discovered a purpose for themselves do so from a background of economic security, but with some real concerns about trends in their environment. The crisis-driven companies are the most committed if they are successful. But the risks and the pressures to compromise usually result in failure.

What about the resistance?

Leaders need to consider whether their power base is secure and what would be the likely reaction of their colleagues.

Frequently, a reformer is blocked by the old leader, a dyed-in-the-wool adherent of the old religion who cannot see the need for change.

Crossing the Red Sea in this event means kicking out the old leader and either seizing this position for yourself or putting in a more open-minded successor. If you don't have the power to do this, stay on dry land and wait until the existing leader goes.

Another typical condition is to have a powerful baron against you, on personal or policy grounds. An individual who will never embrace your new religion. Get your foe transferred to the equivalent of Siberia (or St Helena), explain that he is open to offers, or simply get him out. Moses had no qualms about drowning large numbers of Egyptians at the start of his religion. If you can't do the same, hold your fire until the resistance is at a manageable level.

Consider a spin off

For both leaders and followers who have a cause, but doubt that the whole team can embrace it, consider a 'spin off' move to found a new religion. In other words, instead of crossing the Red Sea with the whole tribe, you may decide to pick the most forward-looking, talented and discontented troops and break out on your own.

In business, this could take the form of a management 'buy out' or 'buy in', a split up of the company, or simply starting a new operation from scratch, using the ideas and contacts you have made (and which you are legally free to utilise) while in the old tribe.

Very often it is easier to do this than drag the whole tribe on a long and arduous journey for which some members have a faint heart. Companies like ITT, Baxter, Sears, Corning, Hanson and ICI have recognised the impossibility of changing the whole tribe and have split their organisations into separate tribes. After all, Moses, a powerful Egyptian politician, did the same. Rather than attempt to change Egypt, he created a spin-off.

For non-business organisations, a spin-off may mean selecting some of the best people from one existing group or from two or more different places. Whatever the new team, a base of personal friendship helps enormously — provided you can share the same Cause.

Once the leader has decided to cross

Those who think they are leaders and have decided to lead the charge across the Red Sea now need to marshal their troops.

Begin with the two to five people who *really* run the team, who are the dominant coalition. Have they all signed up for the crusade?

Should you be open or conspiratorial?

Many argue that if you want to launch a crusade – whether in a business firm, a department or a voluntary organisation – you should take your plan openly to the Board and discuss it with them. They say that you shouldn't start a new religion by sneaking around behind other people's backs testing their support.

They are wrong. If Moses had put his plan to the Egyptian Cabinet, where would we be now? Once the leader has decided to cross he or she must make sure of his or her co-founders. Be careful. The current holders of power may not be willing to throw away their hard-earned gains and head for the Sinai desert. They may humour a leader or group of individuals with a crusade. But they are master politicians. They will know how to kill the initiative before it gains consensus support.

So take your plan to the most receptive Board members first. If you can get a colleague to do the conspiratorial work for you, so much the better.

Make sure you have your co-founders bonded to the cause before you set out. And don't sell it simply as a land of milk and honey. Point out the downsides. Make sure of your ground.

Then plot with your co-founders about who you will leave behind. Some of your Board will not want to enter the Red Sea. Some will actively resist. Even if they go across, their hearts will remain in Egypt. These people are all dangerous, and if at all possible should be left behind in Egypt.

If you prepare the ground well you will find the Red Sea crossing easy. The sea parts, difficulties fall away, and you know you can do it. But beware the early euphoria. The journey you have embarked upon will take at least three to five years and will need cunning, determination and not a little luck. You've just crossed into the desert and all that beckons is the wilderness. It's time to start the journey proper.

Advice to Bob Horton ...

On page 9 Bob Horton's efforts to wake up and shake up BP were described. How could the Moses story have raised Bob Horton's odds of success?

1 Define the cause

We have argued that leaders need to have a clear cause before they set out to cross the Red Sea. We would have advised Bob Horton to spend some time thinking through his cause in the six months prior to his appointment.

So what was Horton's cause? He is reported as having been in 'culture shock' when he returned to BP from two years in America. So maybe his cause was to slay the BP bureaucratic dragon. He claimed to be creating 'the corporate equivalent to perestroika and glasnost.' On the other hand, much of his cause was defined by PROJECT 1990. With its many detailed recommendations it was a blueprint more than a cause.

Horton was clearly trying to make BP more 'nimble'. He used words like teamwork, trust and caring. Yet he also clearly needed to reduce the number of people substantially and he was coming to the job with a British reputation, earned as leader of the chemicals business, as Horton the Hatchet. Horton's cause was not clear. Moses' first recommendation to Horton would have been – *don't cross the Red Sea without a clear cause*.

To start a wake up and shake up programme the leader needs a compelling cause. He or she does not want too much detail. The *Financial Times* reported 'a burning impatience for change on all fronts was evident right across BP'. This is the ideal environment in which to head for the Red Sea. But the leader must make sure that the cause is one that compels his people forward, a cause that will make them want to pick him up and carry him into the water. If Horton had spent more time thinking about the cause and less time preparing a blueprint of the Promised Land, he would have been more successful.

The cause might have been 'nimbleness'. It might have been 'bust the bureaucracy'. It could have been any of the thoughts that Horton had in his head. But it needed to be expressed clearly and shared with the elders and senior managers and leaders of social groupings. These people needed to buy into the cause before entering the Red Sea and before the launch of PROJECT 1990. Probably Horton's natural impatience would have caused him to underinvest in this critical stage.

2 Consider the financial squeeze

One of the key questions is about the fitness of the organisation to cross the Red Sea and head for the desert. With hindsight BP was clearly not well placed financially to embark on anything on a grandiose scale. The financial squeeze caused by high interest rates compounding high borrowing and low oil prices eventually caused BP to declare miserable profits and cut the dividend. If Horton had been able to foresee these events, he would have approached his culture change task with a different style and possibly a different cause.

This leads to the second piece of advice to Horton – *don't cross the Red Sea unless you are confident of the short-term health of the organisation*. Horton appeared confident that interest would fall and oil prices, as well as oil consumption, would rise. This miscalculation may have been the biggest mistake he made.

There is one exception to the advice we have given Horton – where the cause is survival. If the cause is survival, the Red Sea can be approached even with a weak or dying organisation. Normally there is no alternative. But we don't think Horton could have won support for a 'survival' cause in 1989 or 1990. The past success of BP would have made the 'survival' logic too improbable.

3 Be more conspiratorial with the board

The leader has a duty to make sure that the founding group, the power group who are going to found the new religion, is fully behind the cause and the need to move into the Sinai Desert. Bob Horton seems to have given it insufficient attention.

Horton should have considered carefully where the power lay in his management team and on his board of directors. He should then have made sure that all the holders of power were either supporting him fully or removed.

Often, the founding of a new corporate religion has had to wait until certain powerful individuals have left the Board. Horton might have been wise to have assessed the degree of latent opposition and waited for a better moment to cross the Red Sea.

The third piece of advice is therefore *don't cross the Red Sea unless you have a quorum of support*. When the chips are down, you must be able to outmanoeuvre your enemies.

4   *Don't produce a vision and values statement*

Leaders seeking to found a new order should not attempt to develop a vision or a set of detailed values until much later in the journey. This should happen after the Red Sea has been crossed, and after a tribe has been formed. The vision, mission or philosophy statements should not be produced until the journey is half complete – until the visit to Mount Sinai.

Horton should have been told that it would be madness to issue his vision and values statements on the road to Red Sea. Think of his people about to plunge into a momentous decision to change the way the organisation is being run; about to commit to a cause they know to be right; about to let loose all these pent-up emotions; and he asks them to stop and read the small print of a vision and values statement.

At this stage his people are only just coming to terms with the excitement of having a leader who will change things. They have not thought about what they agree with or disagree with. As they read the well-cast phrases, they feel some flashes of warmth and inspiration. But they also feel some shocks of uncertainty and confusion, even strong disagreement. They start to hesitate. They decide that they ought to wait and see how things turn out. They stand on the shoreline wondering if the advance group are going to make it across and worrying about what is on the other side.

The fourth piece of advice to Horton is one of patience. *Remember you are founding a corporate religion. Don't produce tablets of stone until you have visited Mount Sinai.*

Chapter 3

Form a Tribe!

A patience primer for leaders

Moses never read *The One Minute Manager*. In a way this was a serious handicap, because after crossing the Red Sea he failed to capitalise on his coup and march straight into the Promised Land, as today's forward thrusting management gurus would surely have counselled.

Instead, Moses was guilty of hanging about in the Wilderness for an awfully long time. What exactly did he think he was up to?

He was forming a tribe. Making sure the people were ready. And thinking seriously about what sort of religion was appropriate.

This is getting to know your people, those who have daily dealings with your firm and those whom you see more occasionally but who are still important to it.

The most important thing is to find out why your tribe is special, and what its unique destiny will be.

But you also need to look around you at marauding tribes and wild animals that are competing for the manna falling from heaven.

Forming a tribe takes time. Since you are a leader you are probably getting impatient. You're not used to things that have a time horizon longer than a year or two. You're also frustrated because we're not telling you in detail what you actually have to do to form a tribe. Hang on, we're just about to. But beware: this is the longest chapter in the book. There is a lot to do.

Remember that 40 years in the wilderness led to two religions that have stood the test of time. Take a bit longer than you were planning to (though modern leaders do not normally get 40 years) and yours may last for several generations too.

> *Then Moses led Israel onward from the Red Sea, and they went into the wilderness of Cur ... Then they came Elim, and they encamped there by the water. They set out from Elim, and all the congregation of the people of Israel came to the wilderness of Sin ... and the people of Israel murmured against Moses and Aaron in the wilderness, and said to them, 'Would that we had died by the hand of the Lord in the land of Egypt, where we sat by the fleshpots and ate bread to the full; for you have brought us out into this wilderness to kill this whole assembly with hunger.'*
>
> *Then the Lord said to Moses, 'Behold, I will rain bread from heaven for you; and the people shall go out and gather a day's portion every day, that I may prove them, whether they walk in my law or not ...'*
>
> *... And in the morning dew lay round about the camp. And when the dew had gone, there was on the face of the wilderness a fine, flake-like thing ... it was like coriander seed, white, and the taste of it was like wafers made with honey ...*
>
> *... All the congregation of the people of Israel moved on from the wilderness of Sin by stages, according to the commandment of the Lord, and camped at Rephidim ...*
>
> *Moses chose able men out of all of Israel, and made them heads over the people, rulers of thousands, of hundreds, of fifties, and of tens. And they judged the people at all times; hard cases they brought to Moses, but any small matter they decided themselves ...*
>
> (From *Exodus*, Chapters 15–18.)

Danger ahead for followers

For you followers, this is the most tedious and potentially dangerous part of the journey. Your leaders will appear to be going in ever-decreasing (or increasing) circles, and frankly that's because they don't have a clear idea of what they're doing (they've never done it before). You will be tempted to defect. Be patient, though. You'll get there eventually. And it will be worthwhile. In the meantime, keep your head down.

The leader's step by step guide to forming a tribe

The most important thing you can do as a leader 'in the desert' is to work among and walk among your people. Think operations. Define real problems that need real solutions. Moses had to worry about starvation. Your problem may be poor customer service, high factory costs, a bad safety record, low product quality. Whatever it is start working on it. Get your hands dirty. Set up task forces and project teams to make things happen.

You must guard against having your head in the clouds. You must get close to the heartbeat of the people and their problems.

At times you will have your cause to guide you. Certainly the first projects that you initiate must be ones that will support your cause. But you will need to get closer to the organisation than table thumping or evangelising.

Once you have started solving problems; changing things for the better; demonstrating that your cause is not just ego, that you are prepared to do something; you need also to find some quiet time with your co-founders. Disconnect the telephones and prepare for a number of sessions together (at least four) to cover the following four subjects: History; Strategy; Stakeholder Needs and Wishes; and Shared Values. You will also need a final session here in the wilderness to summarise and integrate what you have learnt as a group of founders.

Ind Coope Burton Brewery: forming a tribe

When David Cox took over as managing director of Ind Coope Burton Brewery (ICBB), one of Britain's largest breweries, he faced tough problems. The beer market had stopped growing; lager was taking share away from the traditional beers which were ICBB's focus; and new trade channels such as supermarkets, where ICBB was not strong, were becoming more important. ICBB was steeped in its history. Cox saw the need for a major shake up and resolved to tackle the issue.

David Cox did not spend long hesitating on the banks of the Red Sea. But he did spend long enough to make sure that he had a *cause* that would win the hearts of his people. ICBB was an old site with many of the inconveniences of old buildings, poor layout, strong unions, job demarcation, poor industrial relations, overmanning and underinvestment that accompany such places. Clearly a cause to rejuvenate the site would be one most managers and employees would support. Moreover, during 1982 the chief engineer had run a working party looking at practical ways 'of providing more efficient and satisfying work by combining various work functions within ICBB'.

The chief engineer's report was ambitious. It visualised only three levels of non-management employee – technician, tradesman/operator and support. And there seemed to be some enthusiasm for moving to this vision as a way of bringing industrial harmony to the site.

David Cox therefore chose a cause that would tap into the years of frustration and difficulty managers and employees had been feeling as well as the emerging enthusiasm for a new way of working. His cause was a 'greenfield brewery'. And he launched a project GABB (Greenfield Assessment Burton Brewery). He put all of the 15 senior managers on the project team, asked them to report within six months and asked them to develop a greenfield model for Burton Breweries.

Having taken the brewery across the Red Sea, David Cox's next decision was important in helping to bind together his co-founders. He remained deliberately detached from the project, allowing the team to come up with their own plan. His main contribution was to keep explaining to them that there were *no* constraints. If the plan was good, he would raise the money for it.

The final presentation of the project team was bold and imaginative. They recommended turning the existing site upside down, changing products, changing work practices, in fact changing almost everything except the location.

Fig. 2 The full ICBB organisation structure diagram.

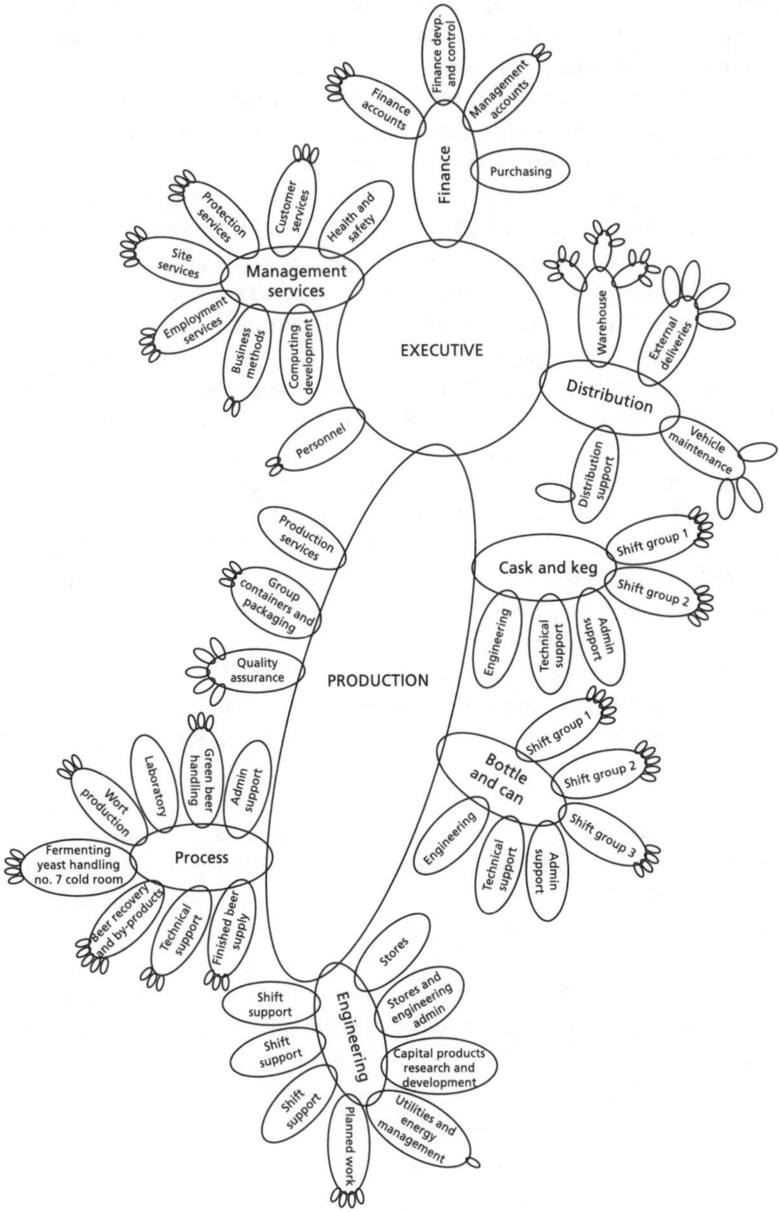

David Cox's next step was to communicate the vastness of the planned changes to the whole site and to the unions. Scepticism, head-in-the-sand thinking and resistance ran high. But David Cox's 'manna from heaven' was the fact that his boss was prepared to invest £30 million in the project and everyone wanted more investment in the site.

David Cox then set about building a new organisation out of the old. One of the unusual things he did was to have a project team develop an organisation structure without taking account of any of the existing people – a true greenfield organisation built around a team concept (refer to Fig. 2). The structure was made public and people were asked to apply for jobs in the new structure. All managers went through an assessment centre to bolster the interviewing and selection process and each team leader interviewed and selected his or her own team. Like Moses, David Cox created a new organisation.

The time David Cox spent setting up his 'greenfield' brewery reflects the size of the undertaking. The GABB project was launched in October. The presentations to the whole brewery about the greenfield plan were made in the following October. Implementation didn't start until the following year and took four years to complete.

One point that intrigues us is when David Cox visited Mount Sinai. He never launched a mission and philosophy statement. He never promulgated a new set of values. These seemed to grow out of the changes and new culture as they evolved.

Would he have been more successful more quickly if he had formally visited Mount Sinai two or three years into the process? Probably.

The new culture and values emerged from the work of the GABB project team and the implementation task forces. Each developed principles to guide their work. These principles then became enshrined in the implementation process. Principles like teamwork were made very public via training and communication booklets. But other principles remained implicit rather than explicit, and therefore took longer to percolate through the organisation than perhaps they needed to.

Each stage in the process must be addressed. Often this appears to slow things down. But in this case, a proper visit to Mount Sinai during the implementation phase would have speeded things up considerably, giving new impetus to the change process and stamping the principles and values of the Greenfield Brewery on tablets of stone.

1   *Team history*

The first meeting you should have with your co-founders is to review the team's history. Get yourselves in the mood. This is not like a normal meeting. Leave reason on one side. Religion isn't a rational thing. It's about belief, passion, commitment, values. So relax. Back off. Give free rein to the intuitive, creative, irrational right part of your brain.

These and thousands of other foresighted founders could come back from retirement or the grave and instantly recognise their companies. The people and surroundings would be different, but the soul would be the same.

Heroes of any kind are out of fashion these days. Strong leaders are often viewed as more trouble than they are worth, with the examples of Ernest Saunders, Robert Maxwell, Tiny Rowland and Asil Nadir fresh in the British memory. The few remaining 'tycoons' such as Rupert Murdoch now spend much time and money avoiding the limelight. The watchwords of the 1990s are teamwork and empowerment, so the praise of corporate heroes may be viewed with scorn and suspicion.

Some questions to answer on team history

- Who set up the team, and why? When did it really take off? Why has it outlived so many of its competitors? When did it take major risks? When did they pay off? When did the company fall flat on its face?
- When were the major crises? Who pointed the way forward, and what were his values? How did systems of reward and punishment evolve?
- Did the character of the team change fundamentally at one point? When did it stop being a 'family' matter? Acquire or lose its entrepreneurial drive? Submit (poor thing) to 'professional management'? When did it reach certain landmarks which it felt to be important, like thresholds of size?
- When did it require major injections of outside finance? What were the strings attached?
- When did it stop being a 'local' team? Become national? Aspire to a global canvas?

Some people who formed a tribe

- *Wendy and Raymond Ackerman*, founders of Pick 'n' Pay supermarkets in South Africa, who fought apartheid, raised the dignity of all employees, and created a very profitable and dominant business out of nothing
- *Marvin Bower* of McKinsey, who made everyone in the Firm (it always has a capital F in McKinsey, like God or Him in the Bible) put clients' interests ahead of the Firm's
- *Richard Branson*, whose style of managing has remained entrepreneurial and informal despite Virgin's large size today
- *Jan Carlsson*, saviour of Scandinavian airline SAS, who focused his front line staff on the 'moments of truth' where superior service can be offered unexpectedly
- *Paul Carlton*, President of 3M, whose 11th commandment was 'thou shalt not kill a new product idea'
- *Jean-Baptiste Colbert*, who as Louis XIV's finance minister founded the Sevres and Gobelins state factories, and can be viewed as the founder of total quality management
- *Philip Crosby*, who realised that 'quality is free', and who through his books and consulting has had the most widespread impact in the quality revolution
- *Walt Disney*, who fused together imagination and discipline, and insisted that cynicism be rooted out from work
- *Keith Erskine*, who rescued Securicor in 1960 and stamped it as a caring organisation
- *Henry Ford*, whose mission in 1909, quite simply, was to 'democratize the automobile'
- *Paul Galvin*, founder of Motorola, who broke with industry practices in the Great Depression, to tell the truth, including the bad features, to radio distributors
- *Bill Gates*, the thirtysomething multibillionaire who has built something unbelievable at Microsoft, the world's most valuable software corporation
- *Richard Giordano*, who transformed BOC from a sprawling and second rate bureaucracy into a true global network distinguished by technical excellence
- *Lord Hanson*, who has been one of the few sincere practitioners of 'shareholder value' and personal managerial responsibility, and who has created a machine which collects industrial under-performers and restores them to financial health
- *Robert Hass*, who became head of Levi Strauss in 1984, led a spectacu-

larly successful 'management buy out' in 1985, and is one of the few turnaround artists to try to build permanent values into the company, and has since become the leading corporate exponent of the responsibilities of business over AIDS

- *Bruce Henderson*, founder of the Boston Consulting Group and originator of modern competitive analysis
- *Steve Jobs*, the Messiah of Personal Computers, who created Apple out of nothing, inspired his staff to take on IBM, one of the world's most powerful and best run corporations, and changed the work habits of millions of executives throughout the world
- *Robert W Johnson Jr*, who took over Johnson & Johnson in 1943 and was one of the pioneers of obsession with customers, who wrote the 'J&J Credo' defining the first responsibility as that to customers, ahead of (in descending order) employees, management, the community and shareholders
- *John Harvey Jones*, who gave purpose to ICI, and whose *Troubleshooter* TV series has supplied a valuable corrective to the popular British view that business is mainly about crooked financial manipulation
- *Sir Colin Marshall and Lord King*, who turned British Airways from a loser to a winner by 'Putting People First'
- *Yutaka Kume*, President of Nissan since 1985, who transformed its culture and the market performance of its new cars, and who has insisted that the company spend 14 per cent of its payroll on training
- *J. Willard Marriott*, who realised the potential to build a high quality but affordable international hotel chain around a simple and highly consistent formula
- *Forrest Mars Snr*, who stamped Mars and Pedigree Petfoods with an indelible culture which is often admired but rarely imitated (what other companies simultaneously avoid debt, set out to pay their workers well above average, and are only in markets they can dominate? Many industrial companies have one or even two of these attributes, but very few all three)
- *Konosuke Matsushita* who founded Matsushita Electric in 1918 and first used the religious analogy for a company's purpose (his book was called *Not for Bread Alone*)
- *Akio Morita*, the founder of Sony, who scorned market research in favour of providing products the public had never even dreamed of
- *George Merck II*, who created a genuinely idealistic pharmaceuticals company, whose ideals have powered it to top world position and made it one of the most profitable companies ever
- *Taiichi Ohno*, who developed Toyota Motor's Just In Time production system in the 1960s, combining the reduction of inventories and the elimination of waste with improvements in reliability and quality

- *Bill Hewlett and Dave Packard*, who invented 'management by wandering around' and realised the need to give all their workers both autonomy and the feeling of being winners
- *William Cooper Procter* who took the enormously risky step of creating a sales force for Procter & Gamble products, thus bypassing distributors who had led to highly uneven demand, and enabling him to abolish job uncertainty at P&G after the First World War and throughout the depression
- *Anita Roddick*, founder of the first and most successful 'alternative' cosmetic retailing empire
- *Sir John Sainsbury* who reorganised food retailing in Britain and created a chain renowned for value and friendliness
- *Jon Sculley*, who was President of Pepsi (prior to joining Apple) headed a crusade to 'search and destroy Goliath' (Coke)
- *Lord Sieff*, who gave Marks & Spencer its caring culture and its mission of upgrading clothing standards for the working man and woman
- *Commodore Vanderbilt*, who realised the market potential for mass transport in mid-nineteenth-century America and then exploited it with trains and ferry boats
- *T J Watson*, who shocked fellow capitalists by bringing respect for the individual into IBM
- *Jack Welch* who created the modern American GE as a model rational organisation, who has tried to create small, coherent units within GE
- *Walter Wriston*, who realised that banks must abandon their administrative focus and adopt a new value system based on customer needs
- *Egon Zehnder*, the Swiss sage who pioneered a collegiate and professional approach to the cut-throat 'headhunting' business previously dominated by the sole practitioner ethos.

You should be able to identify turning points in history. Pay particular attention to its distinctive values and their origins.

Now ask: what is different about our team? Every human being is different, and the older the more different. So too with teams, departments and companies. Your group *is* unique: but how and why? Be especially curious about differences of style, values and behaviour. These are more enduring than variations in strategy, line of business or geography.

How to diagnose your group's personality

For each era in your historical perspective, develop a personality profile of the team. This will be easier to do for the recent periods.

Make sure that you use any data which are available in the form of employee or customer surveys, articles, books, minutes of committees, discussions with any serving employees, etc.

Personality can be assessed using a two-dimensional map, the kind used to help marketing managers segment markets and position products. A popular choice of axes if young versus old and male versus female. But any dimension can be chosen and multiple dimensions help give a clearer and cleaner personality profile.

Another multidimensional tool that can be used to understand a company is the 7S framework (See Fig. 3). Consisting of seven elements of organisation – strategy, structure, systems, style, skills, staff and shared values – the 7S framework is an excellent checklist for diagnostic purposes. Where the Ss fit well together and reinforce each other, there normally lies an organisation with a sense of purpose. Where they are in tension, the organisation lacks unity and drive. But take note. An organisation with reinforcing Ss is much harder to change than one with Ss in disarray.

Fig. 3 The seven Ss.

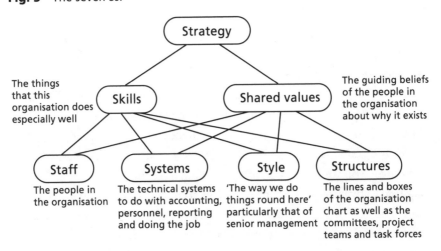

Time for leaders to apply value judgements

Thus far we have asked you leaders to diagnose your firm's character, without applying judgement or creativity. But now comes the irrational, stretching, fun part.

Start applying value judgements: yours and those of your co-founders. Don't worry about objectivity. Wallow in your opinions, your dreams, your own corporate heaven. *What do you personally really like about your team, department or company? And what do you dislike?* Make a list of what you are proud of and what you are less proud of. The more people you can get to do this, the better. You will begin to see groups of people who see the same things. Groups with similar values.

This is also a good time to link past with future by recording dreams. What would you most like to happen to your tribe over the period before you retire? Take this task seriously and do it towards the end of the session on history. Those involved in the history session will be in an ideal position to bridge past and future: to let their ego, ideals and inner dreams be touched by the depth of the tribe's history and so create a vision of a possible, rather than an impossible, future. Simply ask each person to define his or her most perfect future. If everything happened as planned, what would it be like 5, 10, 15 or 20 years out?

Remember that the group you are asking to dream with you are your co-founders: the group who helped you across the Red Sea. This final session in the review of your tribe's history will help to clarify whether the co-founders are still the right team, whether the common cause is still common, and whether some individuals are getting lost in the desert.

But the final session is also an opportunity to find new ways of bonding together; to find new expressions of the original cause; to understand how the cause can be made more real, more attractive and more practical for the whole tribe; and to help co-founders let go of mirages and hallucinations.

By now your discussion on history should have flushed out the important emotional attributes of the tribe, which everyone recognises and no-one normally talks about. The time has now come for the leaders to take stock and see whether they understand their corporate history and character well enough to move on.

Desert checklist number 1: Do you understand your group well enough?

1 Summarise in a sentence why your group has survived and prospered, when many of its old rivals have fallen by the wayside.
2 Name the one, two or three individuals who have had most impact on the group.
3 State how these individuals have stamped their beliefs on the group.
4 Your group is unique. State the things that make it different from other firms in your industry.
5 What trends are influencing the personality of your group?
6 What important attributes of the group do you feel proud of and what attributes are you embarrassed by?
7 What is your dream and how well does it match the dreams of your co-founders?

Clearly there are no 'right' or 'wrong' answers to these questions. But leaders should not proceed to the next step unless they can produce answers to these questions on which they all broadly agree.

Your top team brainstorming hasn't yet produced a religion. But you have cleared away a lot of the undergrowth. You've gained some vital clues about what type of corporate religion the founders want. About what would prove most attractive and enduring. In the next session you will revert temporarily to more conventional, rational ways of thinking, to check the strategy. You will know, partly from your degree of comfort in answering the questions above, how long to take before moving on. It could be a day or a year, but you must feel comfortable you have passed your history exam.

2 Checking strategy

The second meeting you should have with your co-founders is to discuss strategy. This will either be very easy or almost impossible.

Summarise the key elements of your strategy. What we're after here are the *enduring* aspects of strategy, which give your tribe a place in the sun. Just to be clear, by strategy we mean the commercial logic of the team, department or business. This must include a definition of the domain – the lines of business, types of customer and geographical reach – in which you are competing. It must also include a definition of the firm's distinctive competence and the competitive advantage that gives you a special hold on the chosen domain.

For a business, is it especially good at low cost production? If so, of what type of product and for which type of customer? Or is the secret a service-oriented culture, a special relationship with a particular client base? Is it the ability to command high prices flowing from a brand franchise? Or terrific skill in innovation and commercialising new products.

It is not just corporations that have customers. Departments within them do too – their customers are the users, and exactly the same considerations apply. Also, not-for-profit organisations and voluntary groups have customers too: those who benefit from the services. And whenever you have customers, you also have competitors – alternative suppliers of the service, actual or potential. For example, the canteen has a competitor: the possibility that the firm might decide to 'outsource' the function, by bringing in a contract caterer, or close the canteen and compensate employees. The canteen has another competitor: individual employees may decide to bring their own food and stick in a microwave, or may go out to lunch.

Whenever you have customers and competitors, you need a strategy. Firms need strategies. But so too do departments and non-profit organisations.

When you are agreed what your competitive advantage is, write it down in a paragraph.

Every team needs a competitive advantage. The photocopying department needs one. The Smalltown Lions need one. The American Heart Association needs one. The Salvation Army needs one. The Parent Teachers Association needs one. The three-person start-up business needs one. What's yours?

Think whether the strategy is consistent with the sort of religion you and your co-founders are dreaming. Is it consistent with the values you like in the company? Does it help to reinforce them? If not, you have a problem.

It should work the other way too. Your group's unique character should reinforce the strategy and help to make it work. So if you decided that your tribe's competitive advantage was innovation, the way the tribe organises itself should facilitate this, for example by having open communications, attracting high calibre recruits and building a hot house of ideas. Similarly, if the competitive weapon is low cost production, the culture chosen must help to keep the company lean, fleet of foot and ready to turn itself upside down to maintain low cost status.

Beware of an important strategy pitfall: the multibusiness company. If your company has different businesses under the same ownership, the strategy problem is many times more complex. You need to review the strategy for each business that you believe is likely to form part of your future tribe. But even more important, you need to review the strategy of the headquarters team: the managers and staff who are not part of an individual business. What is their business domain? What is their source of competitive advantage: what value are they adding to the business units, why are they the best owners of the businesses, and how do they add more value than other owners?

To help you see whether you have an adequate strategy and can move on, we provide below the second desert checklist. It will need some interpretation if it is to be applied to the headquarters team of a multibusiness company. But it can be so applied.

Desert checklist number 2: Do you have a strategy?

1 Who are your major competitors?
2 Are you more or less successful than these competitors?
3 Do you tend to have higher or lower prices than these competitors, for equivalent quality and service? Is this difference due mainly to the mix of customers?
4 Do you have higher or lower relative costs than your main competitors? Where in the value added chain (e.g. cost of raw materials, cost of production, cost of selling, cost of distributing, cost of advertising and marketing) are the differences most pronounced?
5 Define the different product or market segments which account for about 80 per cent of your profits. Note that 'market' can include geographical markets such as different countries and/or different customer groups or sales outlets/channels of distribution. You should distinguish between parts of your business where competitive strength is differ-

ent (i.e. where you face different competitors, or face the same competitors but have different relative market shares) and count these as separate segments. You will probably find you are in many more segments than you thought. To make the task manageable, just go down as far as you need to, to account for 80 per cent of your total profits by segment. If you do not know the profits of your segments defined in this way, you need to complete a product line profitability exercise before moving on.

Note that even non-profit organisations have profits. Their profit is the surplus of operating revenue over expenditure, or the funds that enable them to expand. Similarly, non-profits have different segments, some of which they are very well adapted to serve, and others that drain resources. Departments within companies have profits too: these are also what funds expansion, or, in the case of losses, causes contraction. The profit is the satisfaction of the user minus the cost to the user of equivalent service if brought in from outside. Don't imagine this analysis is just for corporations; it applies equally to departments, charities and voluntary organisations.

6 In each of the segments defined above, how large are you relative to the largest of your competitors? Are you gaining or losing relative market share? Why?

7 In each of the segments defined above, what are your customers and potential customers' most important purchase criteria?

8 How do you and your main competitors in each segment rate on these market purchase criteria?

9 What are the main strengths that the group as a whole has, based on aggregating the customers' views of your firm in those segments which are most important to you in profit terms?

10 Which are your priority segments, where it is most important to gain share? How confident are you that you will achieve this, given that other firms may have targeted the same segments to gain share in? What is your competitive advantage in these segments and how sure are you that this advantage is real rather than imagined (if you are not gaining relative market share already there must be a big question mark over your assumed advantage).

I have made this checklist deliberately tough, and I do not expect 100 per cent certain answers to all the questions. But the team must be reasonably confident answering all these questions before proceeding.

The first session gave you leaders are rough and ready view of the sort of tribe you are and how you should evolve. The second session has reminded you about the need to stake out your territory and defend it against all comers. Make sure these two views are congruent with each other and don't proceed until they are. Then gather round the campfire and have a celebration before moving on to the third stage in the journey.

3   Stakeholder needs and wishes

The third meeting you should have with your co-founders is to examine the needs and wishes of stakeholders. As leaders, you need to ensure that you really understand the needs and wishes of your employees and all the other groups that have a vested interest in the tribe, like customers, shareholders, suppliers, the local community and so forth. All of these groups are often lumped together under the name of 'stakeholders', because they hold some sort of stake, actual or psychological, in the organisation.

Every department and organisation has stakeholders. Work out who they are, and what they want.

Understanding and influencing your tribe

You should know what your volunteers' or employees' concerns are, and their view of the tribe as a whole. To what extent *do* they believe in the group, and how far do they *want* to? Develop a political map of your organisation.

Understanding each of the power groups in the organisation, who their leaders are, what their values are and why they bind together. Also, how many are floating voters, and what issues will win their support? Creating a religion is not just a matter of principles, self-sacrifice and determination. It is also about political skills.

Some of the power groups will have values that are likely to oppose yours. Others will be built round a specific interest only dangerous to your cause if their interest remains unaddressed. As you understand and influence your tribe, you must start to change the objectives and aspirations of these power groups. You must also lift the hearts of the floating voters and win over some of the cynics.

Toshiba in the UK: a study in forming a tribe

In 1973 Toshiba participated as a minority shareholder in Rank Toshiba Limited (RTL), which made TVs, components and large losses. Rank pulled out in 1980, and, to much local surprise, Toshiba took over, setting up Toshiba Consumer Products, with the same employees as before.

The Red Sea was crossed when Toshiba made the commitment to take over, but the key step thereafter was to form a coherent and motivated tribe. In the 1970s, strikes had been frequent and absenteeism high, technical standards low, and enthusiasm conspicuous by its absence.

In opening up a new company and a new factory, job applicants were asked for the following qualities:

- Expertise
- Enthusiasm
- Idealism
- Commitment

The factory emphasised both teamwork and efficiency. Status differentials were abolished, the factory was carefully planned 'to run like clockwork', and people were asked whether they wanted to work in such a place. Suppliers were carefully selected so the quality of components was higher, better use was made of Toshiba technical support, operators were made responsible for their own quality checks, and employees were given a large say in how the company was run.

By the end of the 1980s it was clear that a new tribe had been successfully formed. The value of production went up seven times, including successful moves into VCRs and microwave ovens, and market share in TVs doubled, while unit costs fell. Absenteeism fell by 75 per cent and the proportion of products 'right first time' rose from 60 per cent to 93 per cent. There were no strikes.

As you would expect, Toshiba UK's speed in forming a tribe – at a mere seven to ten years – shows productivity over 400 per cent higher than that of Moses, who kept his tribe in the wilderness for 40 years in total. Even now, however, Toshiba UK has gone only part of the way to defining its purpose and values: this process is still evolving. Building corporate character takes time.

The other lesson is that there was nothing mysterious about what Toshiba did. The key managers were British. The staff were British. The change technology involved was pretty basic and unexciting. Respect for human dignity, high standards, technical competence and managerial flexibility were the main elements. Technically, building a tribe is a little more difficult than using a microwave oven. What is often missing is the will and sincerity to succeed.

There are two ways to change your people. One is to change the way they think, behave and interact. The other is more literal.

The first way involves conscious manipulation of the organisation's mores.

All great religious founders were dab hands at inventing celebrations, ceremonies and myths to shape their people. Moses splashed out on this, consuming massive quantities of light bulbs for the Burning Bush and a long term contract with suppliers of manna and their helicopter delivery service.

You should also look at what newly independent countries do when they throw off the shackles of empire. They invent instant traditions: holidays (Independence Day, etc.), flags, uniforms, airlines and icons of all sorts. Before long, these traditions seem rooted in a legitimacy enhancing a past that never actually existed, but which is very real and useful today.

Think of the corporate equivalents. Staff meetings, prize givings, uniforms, fun ways of interacting, corporate videos, the whole circus of corporate identity (sometimes useful as well as expensive).

Try to give new twists to old ideas. For example, every tribe has a Christmas party, but how many hold a summer picnic or 'Sports Day'?

Celebrate particular milestones in your group's history, or major achievements. Do things which are slightly zany, weird and unusual, so that outsiders will say 'Wow! They did that?', and insiders will feel part of a special elite. Thought is more useful than money here (and cheaper too).

The second, and more literal way, of changing people is more appropriate for companies than for governments. This is to change the composition of the firm deliberately, either by hiring people to leaven the group and make it more what you want, or by removing negative influences (by asking them to leave or sending them to the corporate Siberia).

This power of removal should clearly be used sensitively and only with real justification, but it can be a very effective way of helping to mould the tribe in a planned, constructive way.

The power of recruitment is even more powerful in upgrading an organisation's character and potential owner time. Planning this means giving more thought than usual to 'group' issues like the location of head office and the siting of new operational centres, as well as the profile of individuals to be attracted.

Understanding your customers

For over ten years, management gurus and specialist consultancies have told firms to become 'customer responsive' or even 'customer centred'. A lot of progress has been made in some companies, and some (notably SAS and British Airways) have been major success stories.

It is therefore all the more disappointing to report that most companies do not understand their customers well. The incidence of customer responsive campaigns seems to bear little or no correlation to either the company's knowledge about customers' real concerns or to an improvement in the customer's perception of the company. This is a classic case of activity driving out thought.

No company, department or non–profit organisation can develop a proper religion or become great without fully appreciating its customer base.

Since I cannot add anything original to what has been written, and since what has been written has been largely ineffectual, I shall simplify. If I cannot add, I will subtract: less may work where more has failed.

Two points: one paradoxical and one practical.

First, the paradox. You can say nothing short, perceptive and true about your market. It does not exist. Your actual and potential customers are all different and would like to be treated differently. But this statement, although true, is not very helpful, unless you are selling big ticket items like Rolls Royces or power stations. So instead we have the idea of customer segments, which group together similar customers. This is not the truth, the whole truth and nothing but the truth, but it is more useful.

Now, segmentation is the most abused word in the marketing lexicon. Conventional segmentation, which revolves around income or lifestyle groups, is farcical. But most of your customers or potential customers fall into a small number of segments (usually three to five), defined by useful characteristics like price sensitivity, susceptibility to service, or demand for high product specifications.

You need to know for each segment what are its key buying criteria, that make it choose one company rather than another. You also need to know how each customer segment rates each supplier (yourself and major competitors) on each key purchase criterion.

Useful segmentation is always related to, and normally derived from, empirical observation of where competitors score. Different companies have different sorts of customers, for good reasons. Understand this, and you are three-quarters the way to understanding the market.

You should ask: do we appeal to the right customers? The most or the least profitable group? The most loyal? The lowest cost to serve? Or none of the above. You need to conduct your own market research to find out what the relevant categories really are, and what each segment wants.

On to the practical advice. To understand customers, there is no substitute for talking to them. Preferably yourself, without filters. Preferably incognito, so you get an honest view. Ask open ended questions. Ask what is most important to them in selecting a supplier. Ask their view of competitors (including your company): how they score overall, and on each of their purchase criteria. That's all you need to know.

Then act on it.

It's a bit more difficult than hiring researchers or consultants. But it works much better. It's cheaper. And it carries the added benefit that you can be thinking about the tribe's purpose and destiny while you listen to what customers think you already do best.

Other stakeholders

You now appreciate the needs and wishes of your employees and customers. The time has come to consider the other 'stake-holders'.

Let's start with the *owners*. Some management pundits insist that the owners are the most important stakeholders. Our view is that they are important, that their interests must be given serious consideration, but that the owners are generally less central to the future of a company than the two groups,

Desert checklist number 3: do you understand stakeholders?

1 Define which stakeholders are important to the tribe and what the main concerns of each stakeholder group are.
2 Do you feel it necessary to prioritise the stakeholders' groups (note that this is not essential, or even necessarily desirable, if you have another touchstone to tell you how to resolve conflicts of interest, such as a clear feeling for what is 'right' for the firm)? If you do, what are the priorities.
3 What are the different 'segments' of employees or volunteers? What sorts of tribe do they really want? What special issues are they driven by?
4 How do you plan to influence each employee or volunteer segment? How are you going to achieve common values?
5 What are your most important customer segments? For each, define their purchase criteria. How do they rate you and your main competitors on each key purchase criterion?
6 Is there a key, most profitable group of customers you wish to encourage to become more important to the tribe? What will the tribe need to do differently to get more of their businesses? What are their values?
7 Do the owners know what sort of tribe they want? Are they happy regardless, provided certain financial targets are met? What are the values of the owners' representatives – the non-executive directors?
8 Will the current group of owners or their representatives support the direction you are evolving? If not, do you have a plan?
9 Do you have suppliers who are particularly important in helping you satisfy your end customers? If so, what are their key requirements in picking whom to supply, and are you able to meet those requirements? What are their values?
10 Are there any other important stakeholders who should influence the future of the tribe? If so, what are their requirements?

The dominant coalition of leaders needs to reach a consensus on these points before pressing on.

employees and customers, considered above. After all, it is usually easier to change the owners of a firm than it is to change the customers or employees.

The owners may or may not know what sort of firm they want for the future. If they are still private individuals, and there are not too many of them, it should be relatively easy to determine the sort of company they would like to see. If they are close to the company and still make a contribution to its life, they will probably have strong views. If they are more distant, their views are likely, for our purposes, to be both less useful and less important.

If your company is cursed with widely spread ownership through the stock market, you might want to speak to large institutional shareholders or stock market analysts, but don't hold your breath. They are almost certain to say they want increased dividends, no surprises, and capital growth. This will not help very much in signposting the Promised Land.

Suppliers can be helpful. They have a perspective on what the company is good at and bad at, and they will know how the firm and its suppliers can collaborate better. The importance of suppliers clearly depends on how many and how different they are, and the degree to which they provide a semi-finished product. A tea manufacturer will probably not need to spend much time talking to plantations around the world about the corporate purpose, but a subcontractor who provides all of his output to your firm, and which comprises a significant fraction of your total costs, should be consulted at length.

Other stakeholders, such as local communities, regulatory authorities or bankers should be consulted only if they are likely to have useful insights, or if the company is unusually dependent on them.

When you have completed your investigation into stakeholder needs and wishes, come together as a 'founder group' and distil what you have learnt. When you are ready, try taking the third Checklist test below, to confirm whether you can move on.

By now, the team should have some strong clues about the religion best suited to your tribe. Take another break. When you reconvene you will consider explicitly the question of values.

4 *Choosing shared values*

The fourth meeting you should have with your co-founders is to develop some shared values. Before you choose which values you want your tribe to have in the future, you need to describe objectively what are the values driving your group today.

Every tribe has a unique culture and set of values. This applies to all not-for-profit and for-profit organisations.

Go into a company for the first time, either as a visitor or a new recruit, and ask the human resources director to describe the company. Most likely she will list its products and services, show you an organisation chart, and if you are lucky go over its history. Almost never will you be told about the firm's values, even in firms which do have strong cultures and which are proud of their values. You will have to absorb them from the ether. Very often recruits discover a few weeks later that the firm is not what they expected, and may be very peculiar indeed.

This coyness about values is strange but prevalent. When did your Board last debate values? It would be either a long time ago, or more probably never. Yet values differ enormously from company to company, have always been key to corporate happiness and success, and are increasingly so today.

In the bad old days, a firm was viewed as a machine, and workers as operatives of 'hands', whose tasks could be defined precisely and who could then be supervised and rewarded or punished according to their output.

This was always a poor model, but it had some relevance to traditional factory jobs. Control cannot be exercised this way in today's more complex manufacturing operations, and still less in high technology and service industries. People must exercise initiative and be relied upon to do what is appropriate, and they need freedom to do this within a general framework of behaviour. Therefore the unwritten code of conduct, norms and values become pivotal. Firms in knowledge industries, and the best firms in any industry, are managed more by culture and values than by rules and regulations.

But some values and cultures are 'better' than others, both in the sense that they work better in particular circumstances, and that they lead to greater human happiness at no extra cost. There is no universally correct set of values

– it depends on the company's history, markets and competitors – and as the founders of your religion you must decide what you want for your tribe. This must to some extent take account of the values your tribe currently has, as well as what will work in your economic environment.

So begin your session together by agreeing what values the tribe currently exhibits. Refer back to the work you did on historical eras before you start. The next page lists a large number of values which a firm might exhibit. Each of you should separately choose the thirty or so values that you think best describe the firm today, including at least two values from each of the categories below. Then compare notes and come up with your agreed description of your group's current values. Add new values in your own words, if you find the ones offered and insufficient.

Next, each of you should select from the full list below thirty or so values that you would *most* like your tribe to have in the future, again selecting at least two from each of the categories. Here it is even more important to create some of your own values in your own words. Do not worry about whether these values are the same as or different from the first list. Confer and reach a consensus on future desired values.

We do not recommend that you refer back to your 'perfect futures' which you developed at the end of the review of history. You will have moved on since then. You may even be a little embarrassed at your *naïveté*. In this values session you are no longer dreaming. You are trying to reach consensus about shared values.

Feel free to make additions or qualifications to the lists. The more unconventional and original, the better.

Some values tribes exhibit

Category A: objectives

Results oriented	Strategy driven
High quality for customers	Social contribution
High value for customers	Growth
Profit driven	Fight for good causes

Customer driven
Create shareholder value
Driven by company ideals
Sales driven
Be around for centuries
Service oriented

Market driven
Goal driven
Knowledge driven
Technology driven
Build an empire
Sales driven

Category B: relationships

Co-operative
Carries passengers
Cares for the tribe
Us and them
Political
After hours social activity
New recruits sink or swim
Respect for bosses
United (all levels)
Clan culture
Fair
Family spirit
Open door
Formal/keep distance
Sexist
Give benefit of doubt
Protect employees
Help junior staff
Authoritarian
Cult of personality
Respects individuals
Everyone knows everyone
Work is fun
Paternalistic
Promotes from within

Competitive
Ethnic identity
Teamwork
Egalitarian
Warm and friendly
Like a club
Embrace human dignity
Conform to the firm's style
Many factions/power bases
Driven by peer respect
United top team
Intra-firm affairs tolerated
Promises to staff kept
Sociable/involve spouses and
    partners
Unforgiving
Gentle
Tightly knit
Worship success
Workers are friends
Tolerates eccentrics
Relaxed
High level of trust
Security/job for life
Brings in new blood

Category C: organisation and control

Visible/accessible top management
Meritocratic
Information goes down the line
Avoid conflict

Closely supervised
Delegation to lowest level possible
Hierarchical
Information goes up the line

Share responsibility
Small is beautiful
Bureaucratic
Management by objectives
Line management led
Small head office
Clear authority/accountability
Overlapping/competing
   functions/departments
Control oriented
Professional ethos
Unpredictable/fast changing
   power shifts
Big is beautiful
Learning organisation

Management by culture not rules
Anything goes
Simple organisation
No real head office
Lean
High overhead
Varied/enriched jobs
Motivating
Led by experienced managers
Different offices/countries
 co-operate
Chaotic
Inter-department co-operation
Excelleng management
   development

Category D: social values

Commercial/simply makes profit
Integrity
Involved with local community
Supports suppliers
Open to outside world
Secretive
Responsive to owners
Respects environment
Strong principles
Crusading
Civilised
Charitable

Popular/close links with ex-
   employees
Ethical
Cuts corners/runs close to line
Respectable
Gives more than it takes
Strong local roots
Drives hard bargains
Revolutionary
A national institution
Internationalist
Enhances society's progress

Category E: style and character

Workers are committed
Parsimonious
Highly productive
Common vision
Scientific and technical
Hard working
Glitzy
Alienated

Opening new horizons
High energy
Work long hours
Consistent
Devoted to excellence
World famous
Seek balance between work and
   leisure

Problem solving
We're winners
We're survivors
Open to change
Beat competitors
National
Exuberant
Idealistic
Time is money
Brings me facts not opinions
Protestant ethic
Fast changing/exploit change/
  versatile
Dependable
Chameleon-like
Whimsical
Attractive offices and facilities
Simple style
Futuristic
Coloured
Deep historical roots
Reflective
American
British
European
Australian
African
Asian
Global
Practical
Multinational
Iconoclastic
Competence and knowledge
Flaunt wealth
Multiracial
Improvising
Disciplined
Unpredictable
Generally admired
Carefree
Visible in media
Mediocre

Exploitative
Inventive
Emotional
Rational
Prudent/cautious
Make great leaps forward
Entrepreneurial
Spin-off satellites
Young
Well organised
Exciting
Worldly wise
Maverick
Discreet
Fanatical
Socially mobile
Prestigious
Folksy/homespun
Creative
Close to government
Visionary
Popular with media/general
  public
Persevering
Curious/questioning
Powerful
Very high standards
Realistic
Popular with investors/
  financial community
Aesthetic/stylish
Smart dress standards
Diverse
Homogenous
Value driven
Exhibit flair
Comfortable
Learn from mistakes
Physically fit
Our way: the best way
Conservative

Category F: business philosophy

Focused/stick to knitting
Diversify
Acquisitive
Cash is king
Long-termist
Avoid debt
Pay well/hire best people
Knowledge intensive
Strong brands
Well researched plans
Opportunistic
Win because best known/
    biggest
Be astute traders
Win because best service
Use muscle
Dominate markets
Low costs
Up market/Rolls Royce image
Monopolistic
Go against conventional wisdom
Innovate

Create unique products/
    services
Spot trends
Exploit political contacts
Copy innovators
Bring quality to mass market
Buy and sell
Exploit temporary market
    imperfections
Create synergy
Good at strategic alliances
Spread risk
Short-termist
Go for jackpot
Win because best products
Be slave drivers
Win because staff highly
    motivated
Get timing right
Win because best quality
No outside shareholders
Turnarounds

An alternative way of using this array of values choices is to choose the 100 values that fit comfortably with your view of the tribe. Then ask your co-founders and even groups of followers to look at the list of 100 and mark the top ten and the bottom ten.

You may be surprised at each other's rankings. Talk it through until you have reached a consensus. If you as founders of the new religion can agree, heart and soul, on what values you want, you are quite a long way towards Mount Sinai already. Before you go there you should have one further session to complete the process of forming a tribe, and before that it's time for our fourth desert checklist to see whether you, the leaders, have thought hard enough about values.

Desert checklist number 4: values

1 What are the most important values, both positive and negative, displayed by your group today?
2 What are the most important values you would like your group to exhibit in the future?
3 How big is the gap between 1 and 2? Is it realistic to try to change the culture in this way? What steps do you think will be necessary to ensure success in this task?
4 What do you need to do (now or in the near future) to realign behaviour standards with the change in values, so that everyone knows which values are now official sanctioned?

Do not collect your tickets to Mount Sinai until the whole team is in agreement on points 1 to 4 above.

---

5   Synthesis

In the final meeting among the co-founders, the team should go back over the main insights from each of the four sessions suggested in this chapter. Remember that we are looking for a unique destiny in the firm, a potential which goes beyond the reality today but which must grow out of it. It is important that you do not proceed to Mount Sinai until you are sure you are ready.

You will now have insights into the organisation's past, a clear view of its strategy, a sympathetic under standing of the stakeholders' needs and wishes, and a ranking of values which need to be encouraged. Check now for any inconsistencies in your findings from each session, or anything that needs to be revisited in the light of later sessions. For example, your choice of values may require you to look again at the strategy, to make sure the two are consistent.

A high-tech Scandinavian company defined its competitive advantage as being its innovative product development. Its culture was geared to preserving Scandinavian values which seemed to lead to extraordinarily productive R&D. A recent review of strategy, however, concluded that change in the industry required the company to grow much more rapidly in world markets if it was to capture the profit potential of its products.

So the company faced a paradox: to survive, it would need to place much more emphasis on market development and internationalisation. Yet the essence of the company was its Swedishness. The strategy required a cultural and power shift away from its Nordic heritage, and the creation of an international management cadre skilled in marketing as well as product development. Some shift in values was needed.

But the values also required some shift in strategy. The need to attract innovative managers with international experience, capable of working within a Scandinavian-style culture, limited the company to high-priced individuals. As a result, the strategy had to be adjusted to focus on the high price, high quality segment of the industry.

Before you move forward you must make sure that your values and your strategy are supportive, that your important stakeholders can be 'sold' your new direction, and that nothing in the company's personality and power structure will prove an immovable obstacle to it.

By now you should have a pretty resilient tribe and the bones of your new religion. But we still have not reached the climax, which is decided by the company's new purpose. For this you and the other founders will need a day return to Mount Sinai.

Remember: leaders should not go until you and the tribe are ready. It took 40 years for Moses to prepare his tribe. He had to wait for the pro-Egypt recidivists and Golden Calf factions to die off and the new believers to take firm charge. So you must resist the temptation to emerge breathless from the Red Sea, charge across the wilderness on a white horse, and end up at Mount Sinai – alone! If you don't take your people with you, they will depose you as soon as you try to impose the new religion. Make sure your top colleagues are riding with you and that you have a praetorian guard you can trust. Check that the stragglers are within range (or cut off for good). Monitor how far the tribe is comfortable with the leadership group and your new values. Realise that analysis is no substitute for action, and that the new values must creep into currency by action and osmosis rather than decree.

The time in the deserts may be one year, or it may be five. If you really are the leader you're cracked up to be, you will know when the people are ready.

Advice to Bob Horton ...

This chapter is the longest in the book, and clearly has many points of advice for those leaders wanting to wake up and shake up their companies. How could Bob Horton have benefited from reading this chapter?

In the previous chapter, Horton was cautioned not to enter the Red Sea too hastily. To wait until his people were ready to be taken into the desert. If we try to define the point at which he entered the Red Sea, we need to look back to well before his appointment. We would probably describe Horton as having crossed the Red Sea when he set up PROJECT 1990. He and his team of young energetic managers crossed the Red Sea in 1989, and when he became leader he drove the rest of the organisation across regardless of their enthusiasm. As we have seen before, the majority were ready for change. So the Red Sea crossing may not have been a problem despite our reservations.

Now Horton's task was to form a tribe. He should move slowly, making sure of the ground.

1 Beware the idealists: Listen to the pragmatists

Horton relied greatly on the PROJECT 1990 team of younger managers. Whilst this has clear benefits, it has also clear disadvantages. The younger managers are likely to be idealistic, however much sounding-out of opinions is carried out. Moreover, the recommendations need to be sold to the managers with power and influence, a process that is made harder by not involving them in the first place.

If the 'cause' is good enough, it will energise the managers holding the power. Using a few younger managers is a good idea. But they should be part of a more experienced team. They can help to generate new ideas. But the voice of experience is needed to make sure that the ideas can be implemented. By mixing pragmatism and idealism, Horton would probably have had an easier time implementing the recommendations.

Even as early as March 1990, it was clear that there would be some entrenched resistance to the changes being proposed – even if only because managers found the proposals hard to understand. The *Financial Times* reported 'One of the clearest signs of discomfort among a few of the more conservative business heads and group MDs is their reaction to the proposal that committees and layers be replaced by informal "networks". One baron burst out that he has 'great difficulty getting my mind around this. I don't see how we are going to create these teams – there won't be the resources'.'

It was one of the idealists who encouraged Horton to launch a vision and values statement: something that should not have been done until the next stage. A more evenly matched team might have restrained his impatience.

The advice to Horton is therefore one of pragmatism leavened with an idealistic cause. *Use the Cause to involve your senior managers in developing the blueprint.* If Horton had defined his cause well, he would have been able to start developing pragmatic changes based on the cause.

Horton's use of PROJECT 1990 was entirely appropriate. But it should have been an input into a broader-based decision-making process. To the organisation it felt like a *fait accompli*.

2   Make sure you respect history

Horton's analysis and understanding that was developed about BP's culture in PROJECT 1990 was terrific. No such work is ever complete. But the team did an excellent job.

Yet perhaps the young team did not respect the historic roots of the BP culture. It could have benefitted from an analysis of historic eras as a way of understanding the depth of attitudes, methods and values.

The McKinsey 7S tool is a good way of capturing the historic information. An analysis with a time frame of 20 or 30 years would have shown an organisation that had a momentum of change already. A company that had changed dramatically in the early 1980s and was continuing to make further changes along a path parallel to the one Horton was seeking. The historic analysis would also have identified some deeply held BP values and norms – concepts of British fair play and of management style tinged by gentlemanly values.

Assuming the historic analysis produced the outcomes implied here, Horton should have used the existing dynamic to give momentum to his cause. He should also have been more respectful of the deeply held values. Moses' advice would have been – *understand BP's history and culture well enough so that you can work with the grain, not against it.*

3   Don't sidestep the strategic issues

Horton declared strategy to be off limits. Strategy was something he would handle with his Board. PROJECT 1990 and the Culture Change Team were asked to focus on organisation issues. We would have counselled him against this separation. Strategy and values are the guiding thoughts behind organisation design. It is unreasonable to attempt to work with only one.

Both PROJECT 1990 and the Culture Change Team found this separation awkward; managers in workshops and conferences found the same feeling of discomfort. If they were being asked to discuss the future of BP's organisation, how could they do so without discussing strategy?

Our next piece of advice to Horton would have been – *don't separate strategy from organisation*. Founding a new corporate religion is about founding a new strategy as well as a new organisation and culture. If Horton had taken this advice, he might well have been warned, by his managers, of the strategic issues his Board took a stand on.

4 *Work among your people*

Horton's successes had been achieved in situations where he had time to work closely with his people – to feel their thoughts and emotions. *Fortune* praised him in his previous jobs for his ability to 'carry out the unpleasantness of restructuring while stirring up the minimum of resentment. He seems to be always moving, always shaking hands, never hiding in the executive suite.' But as chairman of BP he had many more duties and this gave less time for one of the jobs he is particularly good at.

Horton therefore was forced to rely more on his change team members, consultants and immediate reports. In these circumstances, idealistic principles can be developed which do not have the emotional support of the organisation. Also an opportunity is missed to have concerns discussed that can only be expressed in face-to-face debate.

The advice to Horton would have been to *spend more time with your people and senior managers before you launch a blueprint of the changes*. We recognise that this could have delayed some initiatives by a year or more. But we are not concerned about months. We are concerned with building the foundations of a new corporate religion. Remember Moses spent 40 years in the desert.

5 *Beware your stakeholders*

In the previous chapter, Horton was advised to be more conspiratorial in forming his founding group. Having failed to do that, he now needs to take particular care with his analysis of stakeholders, as he forms the tribe.

With hindsight it was the financial community and his board members who proved to be the danger. Horton appeared oblivious.

Moses' advice would have been *it is not too late to make up for planning errors in Egypt. Make sure you have a powerful group of co-founders and understand the concerns of all the stakeholders.*

Horton had many of the right ideas. He later proved to be a great leader at Railtrack. Perhaps he listened to Moses! Good intentions must be supplemented by wily execution.

Chapter 4

On Top of Mount Sinai

At the heart of any successful religion there is an overriding sense of 'purpose'.

You already 'adopted' a cause before you left Egypt: both leader and people decided to worship quality, or service, or empowerment, or efficiency, or money, or whatever. You have followed this cause through the Red Sea and into the desert. As you travelled along, you have been mulling over exactly what serving this cause means (apart from those of you who have regressed to worshipping other false gods).

Now is the time to formalise the cause into a purpose and receive inspiration about it.

The leader must be sure that the tribe is ready to go to this stage. It is a high point which crystallises the religion, sanctifies the purpose, leads to new and firm behaviour standards, and re-energises both leaders and followers, giving courage to go on and complete the desert journey.

It may seem odd to recommend that you only visit Mount Sinai after crossing the Red Sea and forming a tribe. Leadership literature makes it sound as though a visit to Mount Sinai to get a clear 'vision' of the Promised Land is the essential first step in managing change and founding a religion. Utterly wrong!

The strength of the Exodus story is that it clearly divided the creation of a religion into sequential steps. Many leaders rush to Mount Sinai to get a vision without having done the hard work in the desert or risked getting wet in the Red Sea.

The people of Israel set out from Rephidim and came into the wilderness of Sinai, … and they encamped before the mountain …

On the morning of the third day there was thunder and lighteninig, and a thick cloud upon the mountain, and a very loud trumpet blast, so that all the people who were in the camp trembled. Then Moses brought the people out of the camp to meet God; and they took their stand at the foot of the mountain. And Mount Sinai was wrapped in smoke, because the Lord descended on it in fire; and the smoke of it went up like the smoke of a kiln, and the whole mountain quaked greatly … and the Lord called Moses to the top of the mountain, and Moses went up. And the Lord said to Moses, 'Go down and warn the people, lest they break through to the Lord to gaze and many of them perish …

And God spoke all these words, saying, "I am the Lord your God who brought you out of the land of Egypt, out of the house of bondage. You shall have no other Gods besides me. You shall not take the name of the Lord your God in vain … remember the sabbath day, to keep it holy … Honour your father and your mother … You shalt not kill. You shall not commit adultery. You shall not steal. You shall not bear false witness against your neighbour. You shall not covet …"

… And Moses was on the mountain forty days and forty nights …

And the Lord gave to Moses, when he had made an end of speaking with him upon Mount Sinai, the two tables of the testimony, tables of stone, written with the finger of God … and Moses turned, and went down the mountain with the two tables …

(From *Exodus*, Chapters 19, 20, 24, 31 and 32.)

So why should purpose and behaviour standards – vision statements, philosophy statements, mission statements and credos – come so late in the process? Why don't they come at the beginning? Because the leaders will not be ready. Because the quality of the leaders' vision or credo will be so much better after the hard work has been put in to form a tribe. Moreover, it is only at this stage in the process that the people are ready for purpose and commandments. Timing is critical. Let us just finally check that you are all ready to go to Mount Sinai.

The Mount Sinai test

1 Will you be able to agree on a purpose?
2 Are your people already supportive of the principles of your religion?
3 Are you ready to define behaviour standards and insist they are adhered to?

You must be able to answer yes to all three questions before proceeding.

Defining a purpose seems rather daunting. Before you go to Mount Sinai to receive the Word, it might help to look at the religious analogy and at what other tribes have done.

For Christianity, the purpose is to save people from hell and get them into heaven – to do God's will.

How have organisations tried to define purpose?

Four common types of purpose

Put simply, tribes adopt one of the following types of purpose:

1   To serve one stakeholder's interests
2   To serve more than one stakeholder's interests
3   To have the firm reach a future defined goal
4   To reach a higher ideal.

Some of these approaches are better than others:

- Approach 1 can work, but can easily fail
- Approach 2 does not generally work
- Approach 3 usually works for a time
- Approach 4 is the most ambitious – when it works it's magic.

Business organisations provide the best models of Purpose; they have generally been the first to define their Mission. The rest of this chapter therefore looks at good and less good ways that companies have defined their Purpose. These approaches are, however, as equally applicable to departments within companies and to charities and voluntary groups as they are to entire business corporations. Whatever type of team you have, you need a Purpose, and this can only be to serve stakeholders or to reach a future goal or a higher ideal.

A team's Purpose does not have to be high-flown. It does have to be useful to others. The canteen's Purpose may be to provide healthy food. The photocopying department's Purpose may be to provide a service so good that even jaded secretaries (or top bosses!) notice. The high school's Purpose may be to develop each child to her potential. The Cancer Association's Purpose may be to develop cures for cancer.

Any group reviewing this chapter should be capable of deriving an appropriate – and preferably unique – Purpose, regardless of whether the team is a handful of volunteers or a massive corporation.

Approach 1: serving one stakeholder's interest

Generally firms that follow this approach define their purpose as being to serve *either* shareholders or customers.

Many captains of industry when asked the purpose of their company will reply without hesitation that it is to maximise profits and shareholder wealth.

Most of the executives who parrot the party line about shareholder wealth don't really mean it. Sure, it is one objective they have (particularly if their share options are becoming valuable), but equally or more important is a good and interesting life for top management. There is generally no all-pervading desire to do everything possible to maximise profits, and enthusiasm for shareholder wealth usually drops off rapidly at levels removed from the rarefied atmosphere of the top executive suite.

There are some honourable exceptions, where zeal for shareholders' interests really is apparent and control systems built this motivation in at every level. One long standing example was the Anglo-American corporation, Hanson plc, which in its heyday rounded up the corporate halt and lame and restored them to health by a vigorous and no-nonsense regime of personal responsibility for profit maximisation. This recipe, with a dash of asset stripping, worked well for decades.

Listen to Lord Hanson and decide whether you are a devotee of shareholder wealth:

> 'The best results flow from three systems which we operate simultaneously and continuously. The first is the identification of the man or woman on whose performance the business will succeed to fail – the Manager. If you are in very complex or highly technical businesses [which Hanson avoids] it is hard to identify the one person who carries the can for success or failure.
>
> 'The second is financial discipline. We work hard to get our operating companies to understand the concept that budgets are something you intend to achieve, not something you hope to achieve.
>
> 'The third is motivation. I believe very firmly in the combination of carrot and stick. We make it crystal clear what the manager's task is, but don't just leave him to it or allow him to get on with it. We require him to do it. This has a dramatic effect on the individual. Possibly for the first time in his career he senses the meaning of personal responsibility.'

This is what running a company to maximise shareholder wealth means in practice. Could your tribe do it? Would you want it to?

Putting customers first

The alternative 'one stakeholder' purpose followed by some companies is to make clients or customers the purpose. There are more companies where excelling through customer service is an inspiring purpose than there are in the shareholder purpose category.

Marks & Spencer is a good example. One manager there reported that the company's purpose was 'raising standards for the working man'. This rings true for many in the company who remember the early days of M&S after the Second World War, when they improved the standards of clothing available to the average person by selling high quality goods at affordable prices.

The customer-directed nature of M&S (and its touching paternalism) are well illustrated by a story Lord Sieff recounted in 1982:

> 'I got a letter ... from a Mrs Williams, a part time stockroom assistant at our Chatham store, who writes to me that she knows the Chatham area is in a bit of a depression, that the store catalogue [i.e. the product range] is poor.
>
> 'Now she serves on the floor on a Saturday. She said last Saturday she had to refuse within five minutes three customers, for lines she knows are in the overall catalogue, but Chatham does not have them. It cost us £100 in sales.
>
> 'Now remember, this lady gets no commission, she's on a flat rate. And she wrote, 'It's not good enough. Do you know we get customers coming from the Isle of Sheppey or the Isle of Grain, and it's wrong.'
>
> 'I couldn't go down, so I sent my personal assistant, who came back with a report that the range at Chatham was poor. We improved the range and the increase in sales within three weeks was dramatic.'

Marks & Spencer's care for customers is legendary and its staff attitudes, other values and strategies (such as demanding very high standards from suppliers in return for continuity of supply) are aligned accordingly.

I've also studied an American company (which wishes to remain anonymous) where its whole purpose and strategy revolve around customer service. They don't just 'try harder'. They build every facet of the firm around customer service. They enter new business if and only if there is an opportunity to succeed by providing superior service: through being the quality leader, giving the more reliable delivery and shorter delivery times, as well as a more friendly and helpful approach. The firm's distinctive competence is its service oriented culture supported by policies of excellent human relations and training. Everyone in the company knows its purpose and is fired up by it.

Are your customers to be your God? Could your culture really be tuned in to this purpose? Would it work for you? And do you personally and your co-founders want to worship at this altar? This God really rewards devotion, but can be fickle if other congregations sing their hymns louder or better than you.

Approach 2: serving two or more stakeholders

There are many examples of companies which, influenced by stakeholder theory, set out to serve several constituencies. Ciba–Geigy has published its purpose in relation to four stakeholders – customers, employees, shareholders and the public/environment. These merit three, eight, five and five paragraphs, respectively.

Monsanto is shorter:

> *'Monsanto's continuing success requires customer enthusiasm for our products, employee dedication and skill, public acceptance of our social behaviour, and shareholder confidence and investment. Our goal is to merit their collective support and, in doing so, share with them the rewards that a truly great worldwide company can generate.'*

Yes, fine words, but what is Monsanto *for*? Could anyone go to work carrying the gist of this statement at the forefront of her mind?

Mayor Rizzo's number one priorities

The trouble with these multipurpose goals is well illustrated by recalling the election campaign of Mayor Rizzo of Philadelphia in 1974. Standing on the street, you could see a bus go past proclaiming: 'Jobs: Mayor Rizzo's Number

One Priority.' A short while later, however, another bus went by and this one's message was 'Education: Mayor Rizzo's Number One Priority.' The Number 11 Bus had yet other ideas: 'Welfare: Mayor Rizzo's Number One Priority.' Frank Rizzo's command of language and arithmetic was, alas, inferior to his command of the police.

Both Ciba-Geigy and Monsanto belong to the Rizzo school of corporate purpose. As statements of philosophy they are fine. As a way of giving employees or others an inspiring purpose, which runs all the way through daily life, they are fatally flawed.

There are, however, examples of some companies which do manage to worship two Gods, with some success.

The majority of 'Two Godders' wisely select customers and employees to serve. Sainsbury is a good example, defining its purpose as:

> 'To provide unrivalled value to our customers ... to create as attractive and friendly a shopping environment as possible ... to offer our staff outstanding opportunities in remuneration relative to other companies in the same market.'

We may debate whether in practice the whole ethos of Sainsbury is to serve customers, or whether it really does have dual purposes, but it has a very supportive culture and a real enthusiasm for customers. It works.

Sometimes the 'Two Purpose' people choose exotic deities. The Body Shop is a fun example:

> 'We exist to provide cosmetics that don't hurt animals or the environment.'

The Body Shop must be the only company in the world to worship both animals and the environment, but the tribe is sincere and successful, and there is no place in it for nonbelievers.

Our conclusions on stakeholder purposes

There are five conclusions from looking at companies that have tried this approach:

- In general, the best 'Stakeholder' purposes choose one (or at most two) groups to serve. Three or more Gods is too many for mere mortals.
- 'Shareholders' can be worshipped but this is a difficult and austere religion, and only the most disciplined tribes really make a go of it.
- 'Customers' very often provide an inspiring God, but this too is a demanding deity and can easily decamp if your performance is less than excellent.
- The most common successful 'Two God' approach is to serve Customers and Employees. In practice Customers have to come first, but high devotion to staff can actually help this goal too.
- Stakeholder religions only work if the whole company philosophy, values, behaviour standards and strategy are built around this approach, which must be an emotional commitment, not primarily an intellectual one. This is true for all religions, but it is more difficult to achieve in practice with Stakeholder Gods than with other Gods. Stakeholder religions very often degenerate into something believed only by top management. It may be better to look for a different approach, for a purpose which transcends the interests of stakeholders, unless you are really deeply devoted to a stakeholder purpose and are sure it will stick with your tribe.

Approach 3: reaching a future goal

Quite a few firms build their purpose around an ambitious future goal for the company, very often defined in terms of beating and becoming larger than competitors. Thus the number 26 in the world table of drug companies may aim for the Top Ten by the year 2005. Another company may aim to reach

British Airways: emotion at Mount Sinai

Sir Colin Marshall was appointed chief executive of British Airways in January 1983 and helped to lead a remarkable turnaround of the company's fortunes from an engineering-oriented bureaucracy to a customer service-oriented team. It was truly a wake-up and shake-up journey with a difference.

Marshall had no doubts about the strategy BA had to follow. 'I believed that the most critical thing for us to address was the issue of customer service.' The problem was how to take a demoralised, civil service-oriented group of people, fearful of moving into the commercial world and dominated by the engineering function, and make it into a service-oriented team.

Marshall was fortunate to have had two advisers, one inside the company as personnel director, and one outside as consultant. They were able to take his objectives and his leadership qualities and convert them into a journey that has taken BA to the Promised Land.

Marshall's cause was 'customers first'. The simplicity of this cause was retained. But to make it into a cause that could compel 20,000 people into the Red Sea it was sold to the organisation as 'people first'. Much more attractive to employees.

The Red Sea was crossed on a dark night – 11 July 1983. Known in BA as 'the night of the long knives', some 70 of the most senior managers were retired (or rather left behind in Egypt) and the rest of the organisation was launched into the unfamiliar terrain of new jobs, new organisation structures and new bosses. All the old rules of thumb and old relationships were broken.

Over the next three years, Marshall and his team worked hard on the job of forming a tribe. Through training programmes, they personally met almost every employee in the company; through personal leadership they began to demonstrate a concern for people, particularly customers; and through experiments and projects they tried to develop the behaviour standards that would form the basis of BA's new religion. At one stage the personnel function defined some 80 behaviour traits such as 'ability to win the trust of subordinates' that they expected managers to display.

The top team focused on behaviour and on action. Operating problems such as smelly toilets on aeroplanes were tackled vigorously, and a new action-oriented, service-oriented attitude began to take root. The pressure to visit Mount Sinai was beginning to build.

In 1983 Marshall had defined seven objectives for the company, such as 'to provide the highest levels of service'. These objectives had helped guide decisions, but they did not offer a philosophy of management. They did not provide the meaning managers were looking for. It was clear, particularly at management training programmes, that BA managers needed something more.

The personnel director knew that any tablets of stone must come not from the personnel function but from the hearts of the leadership group. So he took them away to discuss the topic. Nothing emerged. It was not possible to reconcile certain important differences.

The solution proved to be to build on the bottom-up ground swell. Managers on training courses were asked to develop a corporate mission and philosophy statement for BA. 'After a year we had 240 different statements' and the top managers began to see the potential benefits.

Finally in 1986, Sir Colin Marshall developed a statement and publicly announced it at the opening of the new Terminal 4 at Heathrow. An occasion of great emotion, it was clearly a celebration of what BA had achieved so far, and yet it was also a commitment to achieve much more. The almost completed Terminal 4 was the perfect symbolic backdrop and Marshall spoke with feeling and without pomp (using an overhead projector) to each of the statements in the mission. It is a day that all present will remember probably much longer than they will remember the phrases in the statement.

The journey to the Promised Land still had at least six years to run. The land of milk and honey was probably not reached for British Airways until 1992 when the company announced large and rising profits against an industry-wide picture of losses and lay-offs. This was a ten-year journey, even though Marshall's cause was crystal clear at the start and did not change.

a billion dollars profit by the same date. A third may aim to become the largest tribe in its domain.

The best role model here is President Kennedy's 1961 pledge of:

'Achieving the goal, before this decade is out, of landing a man on the moon and returning him safely to earth.'

BA's 1986 Mission Statement

British Airways:
The aim

To be the best and most successful airline in the world, earning good profits in whatever it does.

The mission to 1990 and beyond

British Airways will have a corporate charisma such that everyone working for it will take pride in the company and see themselves as representing a highly successful worldwide organisation.

British Airways will be a creative enterprise, caring about its people and its customers.

We will develop the kind of business capability which will make British Airways the envy of its competitors, to the enhancement of its stakeholders.

British Airways will be a formidable contender in all the fields it enters, as well as demonstrating a resourceful and flexible ability to earn high profits wherever it chooses to focus.

We will be seen as THE training ground for talented people in the field of service industries.

Whether in transport or in any of the travel and tourism areas, the term 'British Airways' will be the ultimate symbol of creativity, value, service and quality.

The goals are to be ...

The best and most successful in the field of travel, tourism and transport.

Known as the most efficient, the most customer-concerned as well as the safest at whatever it does.

Sure that the term 'British Airways Manager' is synonymous with people-concern, high achievement and general business capability.

Maintaining constantly improving targets as a good employer as well as manifesting concerns for social and community opportunities and environmental standards wherever the company operates.

Achieving a level of return on investment so that any shareholder will value his/her involvement with British Airways, and see it as an important and sound investment.

Source: British Airways News, Special Publication on Gatwick, autumn 1988.

This was an outrageously ambitious goal at the time. Bookmakers, to their cost, fell over themselves to offer long odds against. Yet in some ways the more ambitious and startling the goal, the better, provided the leadership has the willpower to make it happen.

In the world of strategic management consulting, Bain & Company started in 1973 as a seven-man offshoot from the Boston Consulting Group, which had several hundred professionals.

Bill Bain defined his firm's purpose as to become larger than BCG, a goal which was achieved in 1983, helped by a very strong culture and very disciplined troops.

One of the problems with purely goal led purposes is what happens if you succeed. A new purpose is then necessary, and hubris may lead you to overshoot. Having passed BCG in terms of size, Bain then defined its purpose as to overhaul McKinsey, which was several times larger and had a wider product line than either BCG or Bain. This goal was never reached (in the same way, the space programme seemed to run out of fuel after a man was landed on the moon; NASA became directionless).

The 'goal' religion can be inspiring and create a sense of common purpose as long as the goal is getting nearer. The real problem with it is its collective egotism and the one-dimensional nature of its purpose. In effect, the tribe is worshipping itself. The outside world is just grist to the mill of the tribe's purpose.

Empires like the Third Reich, whose purpose was simply the self-aggrandisement of the Teutonic Race, can be fantastically inspiring but only to a limited constituency. Before very long the rest of the world took its revenge. Hitler would have won the war if he had made common cause with the USSR's non-Russian nationalities. Empires and religions that take in converts from any background, and aspire to serve humanity as well as advance the cause of the tribe, tend to last longer.

This is true of companies too. A competitive goal is too narrow a base for a corporate religion. The jargon of 'strategic intent' (a competitively defined goal) is common among managers. But it is not enough. It can be a very useful adjunct to a broader purpose, progress towards the goal being evidence of divine support for the tribe and its purpose. But it is unlikely to be *the* purpose. Rather it is a milestone on the road. That is why, although the third approach usually works for a time, the fourth solution is usually better.

Approach 4: a higher ideal

Most of the organisations that do succeed in creating a sense of purpose aim at a higher ideal. This involves the firm in setting new standards of excellence, which define the type of firm it is and the benefits it will provide for external parties. By aiming to be useful and to be better than others, the firm can expect to grow and indeed will have a duty to do so. This approach welds together pride in the firm, service to customers and the community, commercial success and the inevitability of growth. It squares both God and Darwin; service and triumphalism. But it depends upon really being better at something than other tribes.

These firms define standards of excellence which are unusual or unprecedented in their industry, giving them competitive edge and a feeling of humble superiority, while requiring everyone in the firm to meet higher standards.

A good example of this is Egon Zehnder, a worldwide executive search firm which unlike all other large international headhunters originated in Switzerland (the rest are American or British). Until Egon Zehnder came along, headhunting was largely a solitary activity (even in large firms), productivity could be easily measured, individuals were rewarded accordingly, and inter-office co-operation was always fraught with difficulties.

Egon Zehnder created a different sort of firm, where the purpose is to provide a highly ethical global service to clients, based on a 'one firm philosophy'. One partner told us:

> 'We are not a group of separate profit centres. The objective is to maximise the whole. We shy away from measuring productivity. You're selling the firm, not the individual or the office. We are very different from the average search firm. It's a sort of subjugation of self.'

In fact pay is linked to seniority and group profits. Egon Zehnder people have a genuine enthusiasm for the firm, believe it is better than other headhunters (though they are coy in saying so outright) and have the goal of becoming the largest headhunter in the world because of their distinctive approach. As a religion, this hangs together well.

It is odd, but people in firms with a strong sense of purpose do find themselves (usually with embarrassment) using religious language. Before we leave Egon Zehnder, listen to one of its consultants:

> *'When you first come here, you are exposed to a lot of strong hype and ethics. At first it seems a bit heavy ... Then you start to believe it, and what worries you, until you realise that you have to have it because of ... our belief in quality, in confidentiality, the process of dealing with the client – that's all fundamental to ensure that you operate efficiently ... I was interviewing [recruits] this morning and I found myself becoming Messianic about the firm because you really believe it. I do believe it because I need it.'*

Matsushita is the world's most successful consumer electronics company. The founder, Konosuke Matsushita, discovered the strength of spirituality and belief during middle age. He realised that he could enrich his employees' lives if he could make Matsushita something they could believe in. He set about founding a corporate religion based on the following purpose:

> *'Happiness of man is built on material affluence and mental stability. To serve the happiness of man by producing products of high quality at low prices like water flowing from a tap is the duty of the manufacturer. Profit comes in compensation for contribution to society.'*

Up to the summit

Perhaps we have tarried too long at the foothills of Mount Sinai and its Museum of Other People's Religions. Now is the moment for you and your co-founders to receive inspiration. Remember that your firm is unique, and

Borg Warner: delaying the visit to Mount Sinai

Borg Warner was founded in the mid-west of America in 1928 when four established autoparts manufacturers agreed to combine. In its early years it was a highly decentralized company running as a collection of fiefdoms.

In 1972 James Beré became chief executive as the company's first professional manager. He had only been with the company for seven years. Beré's cause was to 'professionalise' the company. He improved communications, introduced a strategic planning system, shed nonproductive assets, installed modern management systems and created a model of a well managed diversified company.

But Beré was driven by a deeper desires. An observer noted 'Beré had strong humanistic overtones, as keenly aware of a big company's obligations to society in general as to its stockholders'. This ethical overtone was prompted into action as a result of the illegal and improper conduct by employees of some large companies in the early 1970s.

Beré's first initiative was to write to all the employees explaining that he did not want them to act 'in any way contrary to your ethical principles'.

Beré explained at the 1977 annual shareholders meeting: 'Americans are dissatisfied with business not because of complaints about its common performance, but because they see corporations and their managers as too self-serving, too remote, too purely economic'. Beré wanted to develop a creed for Borg Warner employees to guide them in how to be 'responsible' both to the company and to society.

Over the following five years, Beré made a number of attempts to develop this creed and to get the support of his senior managers. But each time he felt sufficient resistance to his ideas either because of differences in values or because of concerns about practicality. It was not until 1982 that he finally felt confident enough both about his own values and what they implied and about the support he would get from managers that he published *The Beliefs of Borg Warner*. In the language we have developed in this book, Beré delayed his visit to Mount Sinai until the time was right.

The beliefs of Borg Warner was a statement of the values that Beré had been instilling in his people since he took office in 1972. As a result there were few surprises. The values were strengthened and given clearer definition. But they were not created by the document. The document contained an introductory paragraph about the interconnection between

business and society. It had five further paragraphs each headed by a
belief statement. These were:

- We believe in the dignity of the individual
- We believe in our responsibility to the common good
- We believe in the endless quest for excellence
- We believe in continuous renewal
- We believe in the commonwealth of Borg Warner and its people.

James Beré had clearly set out on a journey to make Borg Warner a company people could believe in.

what may have worked for others may not be your destiny. Now you must
step forward and define your Purpose, the heart of your new religion.

Have you all heard the Word? Are your transcriptions the same? Are you
sure it will work? Hallelujah!

But before you return to the tribe with the glad tidings, don't forget the
tablets of stone, the Ten Commandments that will help you communicate
your new religion.

The Ten Commandments

Purpose is no good unless it is converted into action. Action means behaviour guidelines that tell people when to start doing differently on Monday
morning. Hence the need for the Ten Commandments.

It's a curious thing, but they all come back from Mount Sinai with a different set of commandments. Except for the first, which is always the same:

'You shall have no other Gods besides me.'

In other words, having established the group's purpose, you and your tribe
must stick to it, and not go whoring after false gods or the latest fad.

After this commandment, the list varies and so does the length, so although there are conventionally ten commandments, some religions having

many more, and others make do with just two. As Saint Augustine said, 'Love God [serve the purpose], and do what you like.' The American retailer Nordstrom has two commandments. The first is 'Do whatever you think appropriate given the situation'; and the second commandment is 'There are no other rules.'

Ten is a good number, however, and unless you leaders find it too artificial, we suggest you try to define the most important ten, or rather nine, since having defined the corporate purpose the first commandment is to serve that.

The leaders' guide to receiving the Ten Commandments

When all of the top team have read the following guidelines, divide up the task and get each of your fellow leaders to compose four commandments. You should then come together to discuss, amend and select the top ten.

Remember your discussions on values and strategy and look up your notes on these. Each commandment should be consistent not only with the new purpose, but also with the values and strategy.

Some other more specific guidelines:

- *Each commandment must either prohibit or command some particular type of behaviour in such a way that there is no doubt what is meant*, and so that an objective review of behaviour would have no difficulty in saying whether or not the commandment had been met.

  For example, a commandment which would fail this test would be: 'Show concern about your subordinates' career development and give frequent feedback on performance', since perceptions of whether this had been met could legitimately vary.

  A commandment which would pass this test would instead be: 'Hold performance appraisals at least twice a year and identify at least two specific possible next jobs for which the person is to be groomed.'

- *Each commandment must have a clear link to the group purpose.* For example, if the purpose is to provide the best customer service for office products in California, commandments which would link into the purpose would include: 'All customer complaints must be logged by the person receiving them, whatever his or her job function, and that person must ensure that remedial action has been taken within 24 hours', or: 'All staff shall receive customer service training for at least two weeks before being allowed near customers'. Examples of commandments not clearly linking into the corporate purpose would be: 'Service engineers must make at least four service calls a day', or 'All service staff shall receive job descriptions and fulfil them'.
- *The tribe must be capable of meeting the commandments.* Impossibly high standards reinforce failure and demotivate. If in doubt, set low targets and then revise the commandments once that standard has been attained. The tribe must be supported, reminded, hassled and if necessary harried into compliance with the commandments.
- *The commandments must be capable of acting as symbols of the tribe's values.* For example, the behaviour norm of bowling as a greeting, still strong in Japan, is a symbol of people's belief in humility and harmony. You need to find commandments with equally powerful symbolic value.

Before you finalise your list of commandments, stop and think more broadly what you are about. You are trying to lay down law for your tribe for the next 100 years or more. You are not trying to articulate the latest management fad or list all the things your tribe are doing wrong. Half of the commandments you list will be ones that the tribe recognises already. What you are trying to do is to produce a set of rules that will last despite changes in the market place; despite changes in national culture; and despite the phenomenal growth your tribe will experience in the promised land. Think of Konosuke Matsushita defining the commandments for his company against a background of a 250-year strategy designed to take the past and mould it to the future. Think of a soup whose flavour you are setting out to change. The 50 per cent of your commandments that are new, that require changes in

North American Tool and Die: a study from Mount Sinai

Many of the 'excellent' companies celebrated in *In Search of Excellence* have since fallen from grace, but the North American Tool and Die Company (NATD) has not. This is a high quality Silicon Valley precision job shop which was turned around by a new managing director and shareholder, Tom Melohn, in 1977, and which has prospered ever since.

Its strategies and values are distinctive and complement each other. The strategy is to choose customers carefully and grow with them, by offering the highest quality work but combining this with service, prompt delivery and the lowest costs. Customers must be growing faster than their industry, be 'decent people' to deal with, and pay on time. NATD is also sole supplier to its clients.

The culture is based on friendship, free speech and shared rewards, but also on high and clear behaviour standards. NATD rewards high technical achievement and innovation by a series of rituals and special events. The rituals include cash and an engraved plaque to the 'super-person of the month', doughnuts with the pay cheques, silver anniversary dollars, and a monthly review with all staff of performance statistics. The special events include visits from and to customers.

The result is extraordinary quality on incredibly thin tolerances, as well as virtually no absenteeism and over a hundred applicants for any job, despite steady growth.

Still, NATD is helped by being a small organisation. The headcount is around 100, which is small enough to preserve a genuine family atmosphere and for everyone to know everyone. The interesting point is that even such a small unit benefits from a clear and predictable set of behaviour standards ('thou shalt not be late with an order'), rituals and rewards. These reinforce rather than crowd out spontaneous displays of affection.

Most readers will work in larger organisations. These need the commandments, sub-commandments, codes and policies to a much greater degree than NATD, yet NATD has these aplenty.

behaviour, are like the herbs and spices that you put into the soup to change its flavour. Pick them carefully. You will not get a second chance. These are the commandments that will be written on the tombstone of your career. Be inspired by Mount Sinai. But be sure your feet are firmly on the plains and your eyes have adjusted to the hard light of the desert floor.

Sub-commandments, codes and policies

For some organisations, ten commandments are fine as a starter, but they then go on to define the new behaviour standards at length, either for everyone or for particular groups of staff.

British Airways aims 'To be the best and most successful company in the airline industry' by 'Putting People First', but translates this purpose into detailed policies such as the need for in-flight services to be at least as good as those of competitors on the same route, and the requirement that all employees should be helpful and friendly at all times.

The Body Shop's purpose of helping to save the environment has been translated into policies and standards, like the pioneering provision of two waste bins to all employees: one for ordinary waste and the other for recyclable material.

At Egon Zehnder the 'professional consulting approach' has been described and proscribed in detail with many subpolicies and written instructions. You will need to do the same with your commandments. But remember, the policies and subpolicies can change; the commandments cannot. Hence it is the phrasing and meaning of the commandments that is the most important output of your post-Sinai meeting.

On to the home straight

You now have your religion and your commandments. Both leaders and followers may feel you are turning into the home straight. But the race in earnest is only just beginning. The most difficult part is still ahead: getting yourself and your colleagues at all levels to believe and act according to the new religion. Only once this has become second nature and the new values are irreversible will you be in the Promised Land. The journey has begun in earnest.

Advice to Bob Horton ...

As with the previous steps on the journey to the Promised Land, let's return again to the story of Bob Horton and BP. We have seen that Horton visited Mount Sinai too early in his journey. He crossed the Red Sea with his PROJECT 1990 team and ran straight to Mount Sinai. He failed to prepare himself beforehand or take the time needed to 'know' that his Mount Sinai inspiration was not just hallucination.

Despite his hurried visit, Horton did come down from Sinai with the blueprint of a corporate religion that has clearly had a big impact on BP. A year after his departure the culture change programme is still continuing and the vision and values are still in place.

A letter from Bob Horton explaining the vision and values was sent to all BP managers addressed 'Dear Colleague' and dated 11 March 1990. This was a bad move. A new leader should not offer a complete vision and values blueprint on his first day as leader.

Nevertheless, the document was excellent. Under the heading 'BP Vision' the company's purpose is stated as being 'the world's most successful oil company in the 1990s and beyond'. The main yardsticks of success are the creation of wealth to reward stakeholders and having a management style that liberates talent and enthusiasm.

'BP Values' are expressed in terms of responsibilities to stakeholders with shareholders clearly positioned as the central stakeholder. While there is little that is controversial in the values, they clearly have meaning for BP people that goes beyond the polished phrases. They demonstrate a clear philosophy that is both internally consistent and attractive.

Given the earlier criticism of Horton's hastiness, the only additional piece of advice would have been – *ensure that your values can be turned into practical behaviour standards before you pin them to the wall*. The well-intentioned phrase is the occupational hazard of those who attempt to write value statements. The only way to avoid this pitfall is to follow the rule of never writing down a value statement without also defining a standard of performance to go with it either in terms of outcome or behaviour.

In the BP values (refer to Fig. 5) the easy sentence to pick on is the one that says 'We encourage our employees to strike a balance between their responsibilities to BP and to their home life'. What does this mean? What is the performance standard? What is the behaviour instruction? Is it practical? Clearly for the workaholic manager who chooses to explain his or her long hours in terms of the job, the phrase is an affront. Moreover,

Fig. 5 BP values

The principles and values to which we are committed and which will underpin our vision are reflected in our responsibilities to all our stakeholders:

Our employees:
For every employee our values mean a trusting, equal opportunity, non-discriminatory working environment. Our company offers challenging and exciting work. We will vigorously promote career development and we will aim to offer all employees a challenging career. We will seek to recognise both individual contribution and collective teamwork. We encourage our employees to strike a balance between their responsibilities to BP and to their home life.

Our customers:
We are committed at all times to integrity and fairness; to quality products and services which give our customers good value; and to technological and innovative skills to develop new products. We seek to achieve customer satisfaction and to build long-lasting beneficial partnerships with them.

Our shareholders:
It is only by achieving these values that our shareholders will benefit from a more productive and competitive BP which, in comparison with our competitors, will yield an attractive return in terms of dividend and long-term growth.

Our suppliers:
We seek mutually beneficial relationships with suppliers, contractors and service industries. We offer to treat them as we wish to be treated by our customers.

The community:
In all our operations we will act as responsible corporate citizens. Wherever we operate we strive to be an industry leader in safety practices and in environmental standards. We expect to involve ourselves in and contribute to local communities and education. We will conduct our relationships with governments and statutory bodies not only within the law but also with exemplary standards of ethics.

given the tireless energy and commitment of Bob Horton himself, it is an easy phrase for the cynics to ridicule.

Our rule is clear. Don't put down in black and white a values statement unless you can attach to it some behaviour-based performance standard. This is one of the reasons why it is necessary to delay writing a values statement until you are well into the change process. You do not know what the appropriate performance standards are until you have worked with the value for a year or two.

To illustrate this point further, one of the themes around which the Culture Change Team ran workshops was the acronym **OPEN**, standing for **O**pen thinking, **P**ersonal impact, **E**mpowering and **N**etworking. It was a fascinating and well delivered workshop. But it was clear that these were new words which could not be given real meaning until managers started behaving in different ways. By leading with new jargon and un-tried ideas, the change team were risking much more than they needed to. The jargon and workshops, we believe, came too early in the process because the visit to Mount Sinai came too early. Jargon and its communi-cation should follow the visit to Mount Sinai not precede. It will, then, be readily accepted. After Sinai it is serving to label behaviours that already exist.

Remember Moses did not receive the ten commandments until after he had been in the desert for 40 years.

Chapter 5

The Long Slog to the Promised Land

A warning to leaders

You have your purpose and your Ten Commandments. You can see the Promised Land. But how do you get your people there?

Or in boring old corporate-speak, how do you implement it?

Be careful. The standard approach to implementation never works. It's like hoping to convert Hindus by mailing them bibles. No self-respecting vicar would do this. Yet it's dreadfully common amongst industrialists.

Conventional wisdom has it that top management writes it all down (or does a corporate video), gives all employees their Little Red Book, and then goes on a road show round the corporate empire to beat the drum and preach the gospel. Throw around a little corporate largesse, hire a few corporate communications consultants, and sit back for the imminent welcome from St Peter at the pearly gates.

This is not how you start a religion. Contrary to popular belief, *Exodus* was written several hundred years after Moses died, and by that time the religion was securely established. Similarly, Christ did not write a book and syndicate the paperback rights. As far as we know he wrote nothing, and the gospels were not started until ten years after his death, when Christianity was already well shaped and experiencing explosive growth. Writing it down is not the way to begin.

So what is?

The Lord said to Moses, 'Send men to spy out the land of Canaan, which I give to the people of Israel.' ... Moses sent them to spy out the land ... and said to them, 'Go up into the Negeb yonder, and go up into the hill country, and see what the land is, and whether the people who dwell in it are strong or weak ...'

At the end of forty days they returned from spying out the land ... and they told him, 'We came to the land to which you sent us; it flows with milk and honey, and this is its fruit. Yet the people who dwell in the land are strong; and the cities are fortified and very large; and besides, we saw the descendants of Anak there ...'

Then all the congregation raised a loud cry; and the people wept that night. And all the people of Israel murmured against Moses and Aaron ... and they said to one another, 'Let us choose a captain, and go back to Egypt.' Then ... Joshua and Caleb, who were among those who had spied out the land, rent their clothes, and said to the people of Israel, 'The land, which we passed through to spy it out, is an exceedingly good land. If the Lord delights in us, he will bring us into this land and give it to us, and land which flows with milk and honey. Only, do not rebel against the Lord, and do not fear the people of the land ...' But all the congregation said to stone them with stones.

Then the glory of the Lord appeared ... and the Lord said to Moses, 'How long will this people despise me? And how long will they not believe me, in spite of all the signs which I have wrought amongst them? I will strike them with pestilence and disease ...'

But Moses said to the Lord, 'Then the Egyptians will hear of it ... And now, I pray thee, let the power of the Lord be as great as thou hast promised, saying "the Lord is slow to anger, and abounding in steadfast love" ... Pardon the inquity of this people ...'

Then the Lord said, 'I have pardoned, according to your word ...'

Thus Israel dwelt in the land of the Amorites ... Then the people of Israel set out and encamped in the plains of Moab beyond the Jordan at Jericho ...

(From *Numbers*, Chapters 13, 14, 21 and 22.)

Ten guidelines for leaders

1 Choose a route

Where do you start, O Leader?

Be yourself. Work along the path which is close at hand, which you know well, and which leads in the right general direction. Start identifying some operating problems which stand in the way of the new corporate purpose and values, and get the group to work out how to solve them. Don't plan the whole route from scratch; take it a section at a time. At British Airways, one of the early actions Sir Colin Marshall took was to focus on the problem of the smell made by the toilets in the aircraft. One piece of mythology is that he had senior managers scrubbing out toilets to help find out what the problem was. With this kind of focus, you can win small victories over the forces of evil and reinforce commitment to the long march ahead by means of a little shared success in battle.

2 Assess the difficulty of the terrain

Is the path to the Promised Land gently undulating, mainly downhill, well signposted and well policed? Or is it uphill, scrubby, mountainous, uncharted and full of bandits?

Where the values and objectives of the new religion are not radically different from before, the chances of success are good and the danger of rejection is reduced. If the new religion is in many ways a refinement and better version of the old, you can expect it to spread naturally as it creates a new unity and common view. Christianity may or may not have been an improvement on Judaism, but it spread rapidly amongst first-century Jews (faster than among non-Jews) partly because it was quite similar.

Groups are very often transformed most effectively when this happens by stealth, when few people realise a new religion is abroad, and it all happens 'insensibly', by small degrees. The new religion grows up with the team, and is only defined clearly after it has been successfully established, for the help of future generations.

On the other hand, if the new religion marks a sharp departure from the established practice, this will need to be imposed piece by piece and policed until the new practices become second nature.

So before you do anything, work out the extent of the task ahead and whether to adopt a 'softly softly' or a high profile campaign. In business-speak, develop a change strategy.

3 Create the theme music

If you are lucky, the trip to Mount Sinai will have given you not just a new corporate purpose but a snappy way (or ways) of expressing it. Short phrases create the theme music that will stick in people's heads. Try to make the theme action oriented, so that it implies certain new kinds of behaviour. Good examples from others include 'The Pursuit of Quality', 'Putting People First', and 'We Try Harder'. Fresh and unique theme music sells best.

Change the theme music to match the terrain. You may want to have a series of little campaigns with definite but limited purposes, to be tackled in succession.

4 Start with actions not words

Don't tell your organisation what you plan to do. Do it, and then explain what you have done and why. It's easy for the leader to pontificate. It's easy for the troops to reciprocate with cynicism. Start to do things which are at the heart of the new religion, before you start to preach. Remember the parable of the Good Samaritan. You will be judged by your actions.

One firm created task forces employing 100 managers, who spent a year developing a new religion that was blessed by top management and then promulgated with great pomp and circumstance. It died out shortly thereafter. By contrast one of the most successful companies *never* developed a mission statement, defined a philosophy, initiated a quality circle, or launched any other programme. Instead, it created tangible examples within the company of how it wanted to run its business.

Example must start from the top. The leaders must be seen to follow the Ten Commandments before they start preaching them. Consider the arrival of Alan Jackson as successor to Sir Owen Green at BTR. The company is renowned for a religion aimed at efficiency and productivity. Frugality is highly valued. Jackson needs a company car on his arrival, so he takes a car that was being replaced by one of his managers. It is four years old and has done over 100,000 miles. This is placing action before words.

You'll need to get your hands dirty. Get involved wherever the problem is. At British Airways it was toilets. In the canteen it might be the washing up. In the photocopy department it might be the order process. At school it might be the attention teachers are giving to homework. In a charity it might be fund raising. Wherever the problems are you need to be there. This is leadership. You lead, they imitate. Don't tell your people what to do. Do it, and expect them to follow your example.

5   *Create disciples, zealots and sin free zones*

Every new trend needs its pioneers. Every new religion needs its converts, and all of these a high proportion need to become missionaries to convert others. Not everyone will convert at the same time (Moses tried this approach with rather negative results).

So identify the early converts and focus on training them and getting them to behave according to the new religion. Help them make converts quietly, by example and conversation.

Convert first the most influential people in the organisation: the powerful, the naturally charismatic, the respected, the opinion leaders. Much of Christianity's success was due to converting key officials within the Roman

Empire. Note that these converts were not the easiest to make. St Paul's great service to Christianity was to place emphasis on recruiting Romans, particularly senior officials. They were more powerful than the Jews and helped move Christianity from a fringe sect to centre stage.

So devote more effort to converting the centurion than the slave, even though it will take longer.

Passion is the key. You can't create zealots without being one. Any activity – in business, in the arts, in sport, in schools, in voluntary groups, in the home, at play – absolutely anything, responds to passion, and requires passion to move it along. Progress means doing things differently, better. This means converting people from an inferior approach to a superior approach. Nothing works better here than sincere passion.

The lesson is plain, crystal clear, and absolutely ignored. If we had more passion, the world would be a different place. Of course, passion can be bad as well as good. But if we want to do good, we had better be passionate.

Those who see business or any other important sphere of life as a process have it largely wrong. The process usually just perpetuates an earlier leader's passion. Future progress and breakthroughs of all kinds require passion, the passion of new leaders.

6   *Create early successes and failures*

Create models of your religion within the organisation, in microcosm: little sin free zones in particular countries, functions, or special units. Make your sin free zones and converted individuals particularly successful. Then praise their performance and make it visible, together with their peculiar beliefs.

At the same time create some failures. Identify the most recalcitrant unit or power group and look for failure. Don't lose the opportunity to publicise the outcomes.

7   *Emphasise the importance of behaviour standards*

People need to have the new religion enshrined in commandments which are graven on tablets of stone and clearly preached. If you spot someone

Seven hazards to avoid on the journey

1 Avoid preaching in the desert. It's too hot to listen and you will dry out your throat.
2 Avoid leading from behind. You must be seen to show the way forward by your actions and your commitment.
3 Avoid making the journey complex. Take each day as it comes. Each step is an opportunity to reinforce the commandments and values.
4 Don't let the light burn out. Keep encouraging your people. Keep pointing out how much things are improving. Keep showing them how much closer to the Promised Land they have come.
5 Don't overlook the faithful. You must be seen to reward and support the faithful, to spend time with them and to praise and celebrate their efforts.
6 Don't tolerate heretics. Some followers will turn into cynics and others will be actively sowing the seeds of an alternative religion. You must know who these people are and you must get rid of them.
7 Don't rest. The journey is long and there are many distractions. It is easy to choose to stop awhile, to sort out other matters or just to rest. Don't. You will be inviting discontent. Remember your people are going with you to get to the Promised Land, not to enjoy the scenery en route.

worshipping the old gods and reprimand her, beware: if you have neglected to lay down the Ten Commandments, the idolator could have you up before an Industrial Tribunal.

Unless the necessary behaviour standards are allowed for and rigidly enforced, the new values will remain unfulfilled aspiration and the new religion will be quickly discredited. Start by paying particular attention to promoting values that already have a fair measure of popular support. Build on firm foundations.

Make enforcement of the less popular values (like external performance measures that are difficult) wait until most of the 'new way' has already become second nature. Point out the links between the established new values and the more demanding ones.

Nissan Motors: still *en route* to the promised land

When Yutaka Kume became head of Nissan Motors in 1985, the company had suffered 13 years of market share loss, union tensions and increasing bureaucracy, and was heading towards a huge loss.

In his Inauguration Speech, he stressed his new vision:

> *'Nissan must recognise that the first commitment is to customer satisfaction. We must look outside ... the market, customers and competitors ... let's create a new corporate environment.'*

Actions followed. A Product Market Strategy Division was set up to cut across functional baronies and provide what the market wanted. Then headquarter functions were cut down to size, with increased authority given to production plants, which were asked to work out their own ways of raising performance and service to customers.

One plant at Zama held Open Days when the local citizens were treated to bazaar-cum-street-party. It formed new sports teams for the city that were given free rein of the firm's grounds. It effectively created closer links with the community. Combined with innovative technology, the commitment that was generated helped revive the plant.

A series of dramatically different new product launches from 1988, starting with the Silvia (the 240 SX in America). This 4-seater sporty coupé was designed and sold by people whose average age was 28 and reflected the new focus on creativity, market research, rigorous on-the-road testing and direct contact with the dealers. The Silvia became Car of the Year in Japan and by the end of 1989 was outselling the previous segment leader from Honda by three to one. In 1990 Nissan led the American *Road and Track* magazine's list of the world's best cars, with seven out of the top twenty 'best value' cars.

A victory for liberating a new generation of talent? Certainly. But evidence of having reached the Promised Land? Maybe, but Kume and his colleagues have been taking lessons in patience from Moses. He has stated that the company is just halfway through a 12-year process of cultural change. 'People think that Nissan has changed a great deal, but we shouldn't take what they say at face value.'

More companies have failed the final journey to the Promised Land than any other stage of the epic journey, through celebrating early gains too much and failing to notice the return of complacency, compromise and old habits. Nissan looks set to avoid these temptations, but only by constant vigilance and tolerance for a long journey.

8   *Build and sustain trust*

The leader must be open and honest as well as visible.

If job losses are necessary under the new way, then say so early and clearly. Open and visible management is essential to douse the cynics.

A new religion requires unimpaired leader credibility. You are trying to create a better company. This may require sacrifices on your part. It will certainly require straight dealing.

9   *Burn a few heathen or heretics*

One of the great myths about the spread of religion is that persecution helps. The great and successful religions knew otherwise, and took pains (literally) to ensure that they were more persecuting than persecuted.

You should, of course, give everyone a full opportunity to convert to the new religion. But if they are unreasonably obstinate and recalcitrant, that is their lookout. It is your responsibility to burn them at the stake, so at least their souls will survive after their bodies have perished.

After a certain point people need to know the religion has changed. The old ways will no longer do. Change management involves changing people, and if people will not change then the people must be changed. In simple words, fire them (the pun is deliberate!) and promote some converts.

Nothing is more calculated to convert a heathen than the well-publicised burning of a few of them. If you do this too early, you will provoke a revolt. But after a time it becomes necessary. Heretics and unbelievers make it impossible for everyone else to get on with the journey. They must either be converted or ruthlessly disposed of at the earliest safe opportunity. In one company, two of the leading barons in the organisation were asked to leave. At a management conference shortly afterwards, the chief executive made it clear that these two managers had been removed because they were isolationists; they were not co-operating. Ten years later the story is still told in hushed confidential tones.

The canteen or office services supervisor, the teacher, the charity leader: they all need to burn a few non-believers. Can they smell scorched flesh? That's cool.

10 Expect the journey to take time

Most good leaders are impatient. You're good at doing things because you're in a hurry and you drive things forward.

But temper your impatience. The journey will take longer than you expect. Supplies will cut off. Bandits will appear. The waggons will lose a few wheels. The maps will prove misleading. The people will be mulish. Heretics will win a few elections. And you will get downcast on occasions.

Don't be surprised by temporary setbacks. Don't lost heart. Persevere. And burn a few more heretics, just to make yourself feel better.

Advice to Bob Horton's successor

The efforts by Bob Horton to wake up BP weren't in vain. No longer by Horton himself, the journey is still continuing. So what advice would Moses give David Simon, his successor, about how he should complete the journey?

Horton rushed his fences. He did not give his tribe enough time to commit to the cause, he went to Mount Sinai before all his people had crossed the Red Sea, and he spent too little time forming a tribe in the desert. David Simon will need too retrace some steps, he may even need to revisit Mount Sinai. The advice to Simon is straightforward.

1 Make sure the strategy and finances are sound

His first priority must be to address the strategic and financial issues at BP. Unless these are resolved, there will be no base from which too build a new corporate religion.

2 Clarify the cause

Simon cannot abandon the culture change programme. His people are on the journey. He cannot return to Egypt and start again. But he can help to define clearly for people what the cause is. Whether he rearticulates it in terms of 'bust the bureaucracy', 'cut out over-management', or many other possibilities, probably matters little. What matters is that he creates a clear cause again. The BP Vision of being the best company in the industry is a fine objective, but it is not a cause that will drive painful changes.

3 Use action projects to create disciples

Much of the Culture Change Team's efforts were dedicated to workshops and communication sessions. These provide an excellent opportunity for discussion and debate. But they don't result in changes in values. Only action will demonstrate that the new order is better and that it will work. Hence the focus should be on projects designed to make things happen. The disciples created by these projects will be very useful to Simon if he subsequently decides to revisit Mount Sinai and recast some of the vision and values.

4 Dig in for a long trip

The journey at BP is going to be a long one. The departure of Horton ensured that the forces of resistance will need to be handled with care. They clearly cannot be bulldozed out of the way. Perseverance will be at a premium.

5 Look for symbols

The whole organisation will be watching David Simon very closely in the first year after Horton's departure. He needs to find symbolic ways of communicating his commitment to continuing the journey. And he needs to be careful not to signal lack of commitment even if it is unintended. Words will make no difference. The organisation will be watching his actions. If, for example, he cuts back on the consultants supporting the change effort, this may be seen as showing a lack of commitment.

He needs therefore to pick a few clear actions that will demonstrate his support. He could personally align himself with a success area or particularly successful initiative. He could demote or remove a particularly resistant individual. But most important he should be permanently on the look out for opportunities to communicate through actions.

6 Be prepared to revisit Mount Sinai

Simon might well be advised to allow the vision and values statement to take a lower profile in the future. In two or three years it may therefore be appropriate to revisit Mount Sinai and recast the statements – making them more practical and reflecting what has been achieved.

Chapter 6

Quit While You're Ahead

How do you know you've arrived in the Promised Land?

Nowadays we're used to a clear separation between country and town, if only because of speed limits and ugly 'Welcome' signs. Less than a century ago this was not so. The town shaded imperceptibly into the countryside, as can be seen by looking at old city maps. This is still the case with a few towns like Florence today. The Promised Land is like Florence. There is no one day when you suddenly discover that your company or group or team does have a common sense of purpose. But at some point you may realise, or suspect, that you're there, and perhaps that you've been there for a while.

You have reached the Promised Land when the new religion is irreversible, when the new values are taken for granted, the new behaviour standards deeply rooted in the organisation's subconscious and when the people are secure and at peace with each other and the new way. Once you are in the Promised Land there can be no turning back; you're in a different dimension. No hard line coup or wicked new chief can turn back the clock. The future, after all, is not the past run backwards.

How can you be sure that you really have arrived? It may be a mirage.

And Moses summoned all Israel, and said to them, 'Hear, O Israel ... For the Lord your God is bringing you into a good land, a land of brooks of water, of fountains and springs, flowing forth in valleys and hills, a land of wheat and barley, of vines and fig trees and pomegranates, a land of olive trees and honey, a land in which you will eat bread without scarcity, in which you will lack nothing, a land whose stones are iron, and out of whose hills you can dig copper ...

'Beware lest you say in your heart: My power and the might of my hand have gotten me this wealth. You shall remember the Lord your God, for it is he who gives you power to get wealth ...'

... So Moses continued to speak these words to all Israel. And he said to them, 'I am 120 years old on this day; I am no longer able to go out and come in ...'

And the Lord showed Moses all the land ... And the Lord said to him, 'This is the land of which I swore to Abraham, to Isaac, and to Jacob, "I will give it to your descendants". I have let you see it with your eyes, but you shall not go over there ...'

... And the nation finished crossing over the Jordan ... so Joshua took all that land ... And the Lord gave them rest on every side; no one of all their enemies had withstood them, for the Lord had given all their enemies into their hands.

(From *Deuteronomy*, Chapter 5, and *Joshua*, Chapters 4, 11 and 21.)

Two tests of safe arrival

The best way is for the leaders to administer two tests to the tribe. First, the Salvation Index.

The Salvation Index

1 Do the leaders inspire people in the group with a sense of being one team with a common purpose?
   (a) Yes
   (b) To some degree
   (c) No

2 If you and some colleagues were together, could you agree fairly quickly on a one sentence description of the group's purpose?
   (a) Yes
   (b) Perhaps
   (c) No

3 Do you identify strongly with your group's purpose
   (a) Yes
   (b) To some degree
   (c) No

4 How often do you describe your group and what it is doing in an enthusiastic way to family and friends?
   (a) Frequently
   (b) Sometimes
   (c) Rarely

5 In your view is your group's main purpose [pick only ONE of these]:
   (a) To satisfy the owners or shareholders
   (b) To satisfy those who work in it
   (c) To satisfy customers
   (d) An inspiring purpose which goes beyond satisfying one group and aims to do something different
   (e) Not clear/Don't know

6 Are you clear about what the group thinks its responsibilities are to its customers, employees, suppliers and owners?
   (a) Yes
   (b) To some degree
   (c) No

7 Does your group have a 'mission statement', 'statement of purpose', 'vision' or similar statement:
(a) Yes, and most of my colleagues believe in it
(b) Yes, but most of my colleagues only pay lip service to it
(c) No

8 Are you and most of your colleagues sure about what the firm's strategy is, that is, why the firm is able to make progress and stay ahead of other similar groups?
(a) Yes
(b) To some degree
(c) No

9 Are you proud of what your group stands for?
(a) Yes
(b) To some degree
(c) No

10 Does your group have definite and commonly accepted standards of behaviour, so that it is obvious when someone is stepping out of line by not living up to these standards?
(a) Yes
(b) To some degree
(c) No

Scoring your answers

For questions 1 to 4:
• Score 10 for each (a) answer
• Score 3 for each (b) answer
• Score 0 for each (c) answer.

For question 5:
• Score 0 for (a), (b) or (e)
• Score 7 for (c)
• Score 10 for (d).

For questions 6 to 10:
• Score 10 for each (a) answer
• Score 3 for each (b) answer
• Score 0 for each (c) answer.

If your group is fairly big (say over 200 people) and/or has clearly differentiated types of staff (by professional training, function or location) it would be wise to test each department's view of the company separately.

A score of 80 or more indicates that the people really do 'want religion' and are happy in their jobs. Quite frequently, however, you find that the senior people in the group are mentally there, but that further down the chain or in outlying locations the scores are below 80. If things are moving in the right direction, don't despair.

If on the other hand there are scores below 60, you have a real problem and need to review what your staff and missionaries have been up to. Commonly there is still a senior person around who is openly, or (more often) secretly, sabotaging the new religion. See if this is so, heat up the tools of the Inquisition, and order a new supply of firewood. You cannot afford to have one part of the organisation having its own values and standards in isolation from the rest; and no squeamish liberal feelings should stop decisive action.

The Salvation Index, which measures the extent of general religious feeling, is not a good enough test of whether you have reached the Promised Land. You also need to supplement this with a test of how far your own particular brand of religion has become rooted. This is why we also need the Personal Commitment Index, which leaders should administer alongside the Corporate Salvation Index.

The Personal Commitment Index

1 What is the purpose, mission or guiding principle of the group?
   (Give four alternatives and plausible answers, only one of which is correct. Score 20 points for the correct answer.)

2 How strongly do you identify with this purpose?
   (a) Very strongly
   (b) Fairly strongly
   (c) To some degree
   (d) Not very much
   (Provided Q1 was answered correctly, score 20 for (a), 10 for (b), 3 for (c) and 0 for (d). If Q1 was answered wrongly, no points for any answer to Q2.)

3 Below are four different groups of five values each which our group could reflect. Pick the group which MOST describes us.
(Make each set of values positive and plausible, but with only one set reflecting the 'official' set of values as seen by top management. Score 20 points if the correct set is selected.)

4 How strongly do you identify with the set of values you selected as describing the group?
(a) Very strongly
(b) Fairly strongly
(c) To some degree
(d) Not very much
(If Q3 is answered correctly, score 20 for (a), 10 for (b), or 3 for (c). Otherwise score 0.)

5 Below is a list of twenty behaviour standards which different groups may have. Make a mark against the ten which you think are most important for us. If you do not think that as many as ten apply, just mark the ones you think do. Do not in any case mark more than ten.
(Score 2 points for each of the Ten Commandments recognised as important in the firm.)

6 Taking the ten (or fewer) behaviour standards you marked as being important to the group, do you think that in general people in the group:
(a) Live up to them very well
(b) Live up to them fairly well
(c) Live up to them somewhat
(d) Don't live up to them very well
(For each 'official' Commandment, score 2 for each (a), 1 for each (b) and nothing for any other answer.)

7 How important is the group to you personally?
(a) It's important largely for material reasons (pay and security)
(b) It's important for material reasons and because it makes me feel good
(c) It's not very important to me, because I can always get another job
(Score 20 for (b), 0 for (a) or (c).)

8 If you compared our group to others you are familiar with that are in the same line of activity, how far up the list would the group come for sheer enjoyment as far as you personally are concerned?
(a) It would be clearly top
(b) It would be in the top three
(c) It would be about average
(d) It would be below average
(Score 20 for (a), 0 for (b), (c) or (d).)

9 If a really important piece of work came up at the last minute on a Friday evening, when you were about to leave for the weekend, would you?
(a) Leave it till Monday
(b) Try to get someone else to do it
(c) Not leave until you had done it
(Score 20 for (c), 0 for (b) or (a).)

10 If you personally owned the group and/or were appointed Managing Director, would you make very many changes?
(a) Yes, definitely a lot
(b) Yes, quite a few
(c) Some
(d) Very few or none
(Score 20 for (d), 5 for (c), 0 for (b) and –20 for (a).)

Scoring

160–200   The respondent shows outstanding commitment to the 'correct' corporate religion.

120–160   The respondent has considerable commitment but it has been diluted by poor communication, the spread of heresy, and/or unfortunate personal experiences.

119 or less   If this is a typical score, your group never reached the Promised Land. It is either still in the desert or has been hijacked to Outer Space. If this is not a typical score, the respondent needs to be plugged into the mains, to receive a huge jolt of tender loving care or a dose of instant re-education.

Taken together, these two tests should tell you whether you really are in the Promised Land. The tests themselves may not, however, be sufficient in providing a 'Political Map' of your organisation. A further exercise may be helpful here.

Drawing a political map of the Promised Land

Your tribe must carry the torch forward in the future and it is important to know what lies seething under the surface of the organisation – what are the informal groupings, who are the opinion leaders, what are the quasi-political factions (who are your equivalents of the left wingers, the right wingers, the greens, etc.)?

This information will be useful to leaders for several purposes:

- to understand how deeply the mission has penetrated into each group's psyche, and where the message needs to be reinforced
- to appreciate the changes in 'doctrine' and belief, so that revisions to the creed can be made, or heresy nipped in the bud
- to identify where training would be most beneficial
- to pinpoint potential future leaders for each part of the organisation, and even to believe to track potential successors for the current leaders.

Once the leaders have completed these three tests (the Salvation Index, the Commitment Index, and the Social Mapping), a clear profile of the tribe should be in place. Even if all is well, repeat the tests every one or two years, to ensure there has been no back-sliding.

What should leaders do next?

You now have a group that does have a sense of common purpose. This is unusual, and you should exploit your advantages as much as possible. Here are eight suggestions.

1   *Use your religion in recruitment*

It's surprising how little most 'religious' organisations use their advantage in recruitment. There are two sides to this. The first is that, properly presented, your group should be streets ahead in appeal to potential recruits. This will to some extent be communicated naturally through the sincerity and enthusiasm of your recruiters, but Anglo-Saxon coyness can hold back the full message. One manager at The Body Shop admitted that it undersells its appeal to new recruits. 'When they join us they are really surprised about how much we do on environmental issues and other [social] things. After a few weeks they say, "I know you said that you took these issues seriously, but I had no idea you actually did so much."' Do not hide your light under a bushel, or under anything else for that matter.

The other side of the coin is that you can be much more choosy about the people you hire. And you need to be. You now have a clear idea of what sort of group you want to be and the sort of values your people must have. With each new person you hire, whatever their technical skills, you must ask yourself: 'Will this person raise the average level of dedication in the group and make our values stronger?' Unless you can say 'Yes', do not hire the person.

Anita Roddick, founder of The Body Shop, stresses that although business skills can be taught, attitude and values cannot. 'We have the backup to teach almost anyone to run a Body Shop outlet. What we can't control is the soul.' So potential recruits are asked seemingly off-the-wall questions like how they would like to die, what their heroines in poetry are (a tough one that for chauvinist males) and what is their favourite flower.

This may seem a little weird but you have a wide choice of new people and you have a responsibility to ensure that the new people will be at least as turned on by your firm and its values as the current tribe is.

2   *Make better promotion decisions*

Similar considerations apply in internal selection and promotion decisions. You are giving more influence to a person, to all of that person, body and soul as well as brain. Leadership qualities and the propensity and ability to be a good missionary for the firm's religion are as important as technical merit. This is not favouritism or politics. The purposeful firm simply does not work as well as it could unless everyone with power in it is singing off the same hymn sheet.

3 Train and develop the whole person

Your training and development programmes should be uplifting celebrations of collective purpose and should raise the spirit as well as the mind of the participants. Reinforce the skills, values and behaviours you need to continue being successful.

An excellent example of this is British Airways' competency-based training programme, which appraises and enhances the 'abilities, personal qualities, values and drives' of its people. McDonald's with its Hamburger University and the training given to the 'cast' at Disney are other examples of customers who place a higher value on knowledge, attitude and behaviour than on technical skills alone.

Whenever possible, bring together as many of your group as you can, ideally all of it, to one place, for company meetings. Your motto should be 'The Whole Person in the Whole Group.'

4 Educate the outside world

Customers are the most important group which needs to know about your new religion. Do it by actions rather than words. If the customers don't begin to feel benefits from your new approach, your religion is a pretty poor one or has still not achieved lift-off.

There should also be benefits for the *local community* and for *suppliers*. Work out what they are, ensure you are delivering them, and then let people know to heighten their awareness of the changes already made.

It is also important to explain to the *owners* what you are doing. Your religion will almost certainly lead to higher long-term returns to the owners, but particularly if there is a ready market in your shares, the religion may appeal to some owners or prospective owners more than others. 'Ethical

Johnson & Johnson: keeping the religion alive

General Robert Wood Johnson was the founder of Johnson & Johnson's current business philosophy. Today the company is widely diversified in international health care. General Johnson became head of the company in 1932 and published *An Industrial Credo* in 1945. By then he had been with the company for 35 years. In the Credo he 'defined for his associates and for the business community and for his peers some of the things he felt very seriously about' such as product quality, decentralisation and individual dignity. These values were the ones he had built into the organisation over the years and they are still strong in the company today.

He started by holding a series of Credo Challenge meetings to find out if the Credo was still meaningful to managers. Burke's own belief in the statement was strong and he was concerned that it might not be as important to others, particularly at a time when the public were concerned about corporate misconduct.

The Challenge Meetings took place over more than three years with a total of 200 managers attending. The meetings were in groups of 25 over a two-day period. These meetings proved to be unique events. Managers were able to explain how hard it was to balance all the responsibilities outlined in the Credo and to challenge particular passages. In these discussions the experienced managers were able to argue how it was possible to live up to the responsibilities and point out events in the company history that demonstrated their arguments. The essence of the Credo was given a rebirth in these meetings and managers throughout Johnson & Johnson felt an enhanced pride in and commitment to the company.

Nevertheless it was also apparent that some revisions to the Credo were necessary. James Burke estimates that he spent at least 50–60 hours on the revisions some of which were major changes in format and others simply a matter of fine turning. For example:

- The word 'products' was changed to 'products and services'
- 'Our dealers must make a profit' was altered to read 'our suppliers and distributors must have an opportunity to make a fair profit'
- Responsibility for a healthy and safe working environment was added
- Responsibility to the environment and natural resources was added.

The most controversial discussion resulted in the deletion of the words 'with God's grace'.

In 1982 Johnson & Johnson's belief in its Credo was given the ultimate challenge. Seven people in Chicago died from cyanide that had been added to capsules of Johnson & Johnson's pain killer, Tylenol. The Tylenol affair put Johnson & Johnson's business ethics in the spotlight and the way the company reacted is often quoted as an example.

The company immediately withdrew all Tylenol products from 15,000 retailers, recalling some 11 million capsules. Consumers were offered refunds for any product they had bought and not used without proof of purchase. $100,000 reward was offered for information about product tampering. Johnson & Johnson also agreed to underwrite the government analysis of capsules and co-operated fully with the investigating task force.

Johnson & Johnson demonstrated that it really did believe in the Credo.

Our Credo

We believe our first responsibility is to the doctors, nurses and patients,
to mothers and all others who use our products and services.
In meeting their needs everything we do must be of high quality.
We must constantly strive to reduce our costs
in order to maintain reasonable prices.
Customers' orders must be serviced promptly and accurately.
Our suppliers and distributors must have an opportunity
to make a fair profit.

We are responsible to our employees,
the men and women who work with us throughout the world.
Everyone must be considered as an individual.
We must respect their dignity and recognize their merit.
They must have a sense of security in their jobs.
Compensation must be fair and adequate,
and working conditions clean, orderly and safe.
Employees must feel free to make suggestions and complaints.
There must be equal opportunity for employment, development
and advancement for those qualified.
We must provide competent management,
and their actions must be just and ethical.

We are responsible to the communities in which we live and work
and to the world community as well.
We must be good citizens – support good works and charities

and bear our fair share of taxes.
We must encourage civic improvements and better health and
education.
We must maintain in good order
the property we are privileged to use,
protecting the environment and natural resources.

Our final responsibility is to our stockholders.
Business must make a sound profit.
We must experiment with new ideas.
Research must be carried on, innovative programs developed
and mistakes paid for.
New equipment must be purchased, new facilities provided
and new products launched.
Reserves must be created to provide for adverse times.
When we operate according to these principles,
the stockholders should realize a fair return.

Johnson & Johnson

funds' are becoming more important to investors, but even sympathetic investors need to know how the new purpose is related to strategy and what the benefits are in hard financial terms. You cannot do this unless you measure the benefits carefully yourself.

5   Quantify the benefits

People in groups without purpose perform well below their potential. Probably, most people in firms without a sense of common purpose run at least 30 per cent below their potential. If so, 'purposeless' firms are using only two-thirds of the person power potentially available to them.

This guess is corroborated by what happens when organisations do 'get religion'. The surge in morale and performance leads people to 'go the extra mile' in both time and effort, impressing the hell out of customers (leading to valuable incremental market share) and effectively cutting unit labour costs at one stroke. Expensive waste starts to disappear. Unnecessary and expensive procedures are eliminated. Over time, whole layers of management can disappear, not because there is a financial crisis, but because it makes everyone's job more satisfying and because people do not want to see the group's effectiveness impaired.

If we are roughly adding a third to people's effectiveness, the effect of religion should be to add a third to the value of the firm. Here's the rub. A lot of managers are very happy when we talk about 'soft' benefits of corporate religion, but get offended, defensive or uneasy when we come to demand hard benefits too.

They have a point. The benefits are a by-product. We shouldn't advocate corporate purpose as a crafty way of doing down the unions, exploiting the employees or jacking up the returns of the owners. Like happiness, higher commercial returns are a by-product of doing the right thing, and if you focus too much on achieving the 'result' (e.g. go around saying, what do I need to do to be happy?) it will surely elude you. Or as Christ put it, 'Seek first the kingdom of heaven, and all these [material] things will be added to you.'

But realise that *if the religion is working, it will have beneficial financial results.* Conversely, *if there are no beneficial financial results* (over and above what would otherwise have happened), *the religion is not working.*

So you should decide what financial measures you would expect to be moving in the right direction, and monitor them carefully. Of course, it takes time. There may be short-term costs that exceed the short-term benefits. But financial results also have their 'leading indicators', like market shares, and if these are not responding to the changes, then at the very least you have some hard questions to answer.

Decide when you start your corporate religion which 'hard' measures it should impact, and the timescale you would expect. Almost certainly you will want to look at sales in your priority product areas. You should also look at what happens to your market share relative to competitors. There will be a number of measures of customer awareness and satisfaction which should start to respond. Also, productivity measures should improve and overheads should fall as a percentage of sales. Within five years at the outside there should be a measurable impact on profits and the stock market's rating of your firm.

If you are the leader of a department that doesn't have financial results – generally called a cost centre – or of a voluntary group that doesn't aim to make profits, it is still important that you quantify the benefit of the new religion. If you can't measure profits, measure other things that are equivalent.

Here are some measures you should look at. *Customer satisfaction* – the pleasure that your users and clients derive from what you do – should be much higher than it used to be. The *number of customers* should be going up: if the religion is vibrant and working, it should be making converts. You should be receiving many more *applications from recruits* – people who want to be your employees or volunteers. And the *morale of your people* should also be higher. If at least three of these measures aren't going in the right direction, the religion isn't working. These measures, incidentally, apply to profit centres and whole firms too: it isn't good enough to be making more money; these real measures, that lie behind the ability to make more money, should be soaring too.

Pitfalls in the Promised Land

A final checklist for leaders who have arrived.

1 Don't drive too hard for fanatical devotion from all the tribe. You've arrived. The good guys have won. Don't alienate the world by becoming intolerant or inquisitorial.
2 Don't resist revisions to the strategy and values which are necessary in changed commercial conditions and which do not threaten the core values.
3 Don't over-glorify the good old days of struggle.
4 Don't stop the younger generation from revising a few rituals and inventing a few new ones.
5 Don't think you're going to live for ever or neglect to plan your succession. Now is probably a good time to retire.
6 Ensure the strategy remains valid.

6   Ensure the strategy remains valid

Strong values, as we have seen, reinforce the commercial logic of the business. But market and competitive reality can shift rapidly. You need to ensure that you do not cling tenaciously to one part of the policy (just because it is associated with the corporate religion) if it becomes a commercial handicap.

Marks & Spencer managers identified two areas where the value system had delayed shifts in strategy that were overdue. One was reliance on British garment manufacture, beyond the point at which in certain segments Far Eastern suppliers offered much better value. The other was the neglect of the benefits of information technology in the late 1970s/early 1980s, when the emphasis on 'walking the store' and face-to-face communication retarded the benefits to customers and costs of advancing stock systems. None of Marks & Spencer's core values have been threatened by changes in their buying and stocking system, which are now state of the art.

'Religious' groups, more than irreligious ones, need to be open to change and to the danger that a strong culture becomes an inward looking one. Strategic questioning and review of commercial policies relative to competition need to become ways of life in the purposeful firm.

Of course, if the environment changes dramatically the Promised Land may turn into territory that looks just like Egypt. Then it will be necessary for your company to find a new Moses to lead it out of the new Egypt to a new Promised Land.

7   Avoid arrogance and complacency

You will be doubly exposed to the danger of arrogance. This is a natural temptation of success, and it can also originate separately from the religious angle, where the 'holier than thou' attitude is high on the list of pitfalls. After all, you *will be better* than other comparable groups. It is a fine line between knowing this and taking pride in your culture, on the one hand, and becoming arrogant and blind on the other.

Complacency is also a danger. The most successful groups clearly know how to do things best, so what can they learn from others? But history is littered with the corpses of former leaders, so don't ease up or believe that continued success is inevitable.

It's difficult to be humble and hard working when you're wildly success-ful. But it's even more necessary. Take the Arrogance Test on page 117 to make sure you are not a liability.

8   *Quit while you're ahead*

On his 120th birthday, Moses called his people together and showed them the Promised Land. The Lord had decided that Moses should see it, com-plete with fountains and springs, vines and pomegranates, olive trees and honey, iron and copper, and send his people down to it — but not enter himself. Moses retired (actually, died) once the Promised Land was in sight.

This was an excellent move. Moses appointed Joshua his successor and the people moved into the Promised Land.

When your task is over, when your new religion is secure, why stick around? Your job is done.

It is sad that very few corporate or political leaders retire at the right time. Moses did. Having got your people, against all the odds, to the Promised Land, now is the time to retire in a blaze of glory. OK, you can become the honorary Life President if you want, but don't try to hang on to power. It's time for a new generation. Your legacy is secure. Don't get in the way. If you're too energetic, too committed or too philistine to retire, go and find another group to revitalise, or get a Visiting Professorship.

Now, what of your successor? You may handpick him or her, as Moses did Joshua. But we live in democratic days. Why not let your people choose their new leader? When it is time to select a new leader, and possibly even a new religion, allow competing prophets to present their manifestos. And let the people decide.

For companies needing a new leader, imagine this. The top team submit their resignation in July, to take effect at the end of the year. The resigna-tions trigger the election process, the start of the campaign.

Resources are then provided to qualifying groups of executives who run for office. They present their programs — their strategies, their target mar-kets, their internal policies, their methods of implementation. The manifes-tos are put before the full body of employees in a series of campaign meetings, in brochures, in videos, in burning bushes. At the end of August, a vote is taken and one team, under the new leader, emerges victorious. The leader than has a four-year term to implement the vision, to create the new religion.

However it is done, new progress can be made. As one journey is over, another begins.

Arrogance Test: is your group becoming complacent?

1 Do you have strong competitors?
   (a) Yes
   (b) Some
   (c) No

2 Have you copied a good idea from one of your competitors in the last six months?
   (a) Yes
   (b) No

3 Have you lost market share in any niche areas in the last three years?
   (a) No
   (b) Not sure
   (c) Yes

4 Have you lost market share in any of your main markets in the last three years?
   (a) No
   (b) Not sure
   (c) Yes

5 Do you have a young staff group or association who meet with you at least once per year?
   (a) Yes
   (b) No

6 Is your young staff group a little wild and naïve to the point where you are thinking of disbanding them?
   (a) No
   (b) Don't have one
   (c) Yes

7 How often does the leading group have discussions that reach a high level of tension yet are creative and constructive.
(a) We have 'creative tension' at least once per month, usually every time we meet
(b) We had a discussion like that a couple of months ago
(c) We don't like tension within the leadership group
(d) Not in the last year

8 When did you last review your philosophy statement, values and behaviour standards?
(a) Within the last five years
(b) At least five years ago
(c) I can't remember
(d) Never

Scoring

Score all (a) answers 10; zero for any other answers.
60–80   You are healthy and still thinking. The organisation is fit.
40–50   You should not panic, but a good cold look at yourself and your competitors is needed. Also you need to pay more attention to the younger people in the company.
0–30   You are arrogant, complacent and a potential liability. Resign now or shake up and wake up yourself.

Leadership for Everyone

Part Two allows you to assess

- the extent to which you want to believe in your activity (Chapter 7)
- how good the current leaders are (Chapter 8)
- whether you could make a good leader (also Chapter 8).

The next chapter asks whether you want to believe in what you do. This might seem an odd question in a book on leadership, but belief is the beginning of leadership. People who are not serious about what they do never make good leaders. Being a believer does not necessarily mean that you will make a good leader, but it does mean that you have the *potential* to be a good leader. Not all believers are good leaders, but all good leaders are believers.

Chapter 7 also has a side-benefit. It may be apparent after you read it that you are a believer, but not in the organisation where you currently invest much of your time. If so, you are making a bad investment. Find an organisation in which you *can* believe. There, you will make a much more valuable contribution. There too, you will be happier.

* * *

Leadership is situational: a bad leader in one situation can be a good leader in another. It is absurd to consider leadership in isolation from what the leader is trying to achieve, from his Cause, her religion. Leadership is not a style, a pose, a facility. Leadership is how the leader accomplishes what she cares about.

Everyone should believe in something, should have some insight into what could be done better, and should care about seeing it done better. It follows that everyone could be a leader. We revert to this theme in Chapter 9, our Conclusion.

Chapter 7

Do You Want to Believe?

Well, do you? Do you want to be part of a team that you really believe in?

The unbelievers

Most people do not believe in what they do: in the organisations where they spend their time. They're not enthusiastic about what the organisation or organisations do. They don't identify with the organisation. They may not even know what its purpose is. They don't like talking about their organisation to family and friends, or if they do it's to complain about colleagues or customers. They don't have a sense of common purpose, or of being on a winning team at work.

The happy heathen

For some people this state of affairs is just fine. They don't want or expect work to provide a sense of purpose. They work to pay the bills for themselves or to support their family. They may derive professional satisfaction from the fact that they are good at their job and can go home feeling they have met their contract: a good day's work for a good day's pay. They may even enjoy what they do at work.

But they don't want or need to be part of a team. They don't care what the organisation's direction is, so long as it pays well and offers security. They don't care whether the organisation makes cigarettes, armaments or life-saving drugs; whether it experiments on animals, exploits the third world or pollutes the environment, or conversely, whether it is doing tremendous things for the world. Whatever the organisation does is fine by them. They get their emotional needs satisfied outside the office. They keep work and social life at arm's length. They hate being called up at home by colleagues or customers. The idea of being passionate about what their company does is an anathema. They have quite enough passion in their private lives, thank you very much.

Where do you stand?

Which category do you fit into? Do you want to believe or would you rather not? Are you naturally idealistic, or pragmatic? Evangelistic or sceptical? Hot or cool? Geared to your private life or the whole of your life?

Do you know? It's surprising how many people don't stop to ask the question. *The result is that most people end up working in the wrong organisation.* People who don't want to believe may be working in companies – like Apple or Mars – that really want believers. More frequently, people who want to believe (though they may not recognise this trait in themselves) find themselves working in organisations that, fine though they may be in other ways, are not really capable of being believed in. You may be surprised to find as you read this book that most of the world's largest corporations do not have a sense of clear common purpose. The disarray at companies like General Motors or IBM has been clear. But a sense of purpose is also lacking in most other large companies, despite a bureaucratic calm. Size, of course, is a great impediment to purpose.

We are all hopelessly bad at self-analysis. Tests have shown that 95 per cent of people believe that they are above average in dealing with people, thus proving that at least 45 per cent are fooling themselves.

So you cannot rely on a gut answer to this question of belief. It's also important to know how strongly or weakly you need to believe.

Belief is not the same as naïvety. Do not confuse style with substance. Many apparently cynical, world-wise senior industrialists manage to conceal a raging fire of genuine idealism behind a forbidding, gruff exterior. In contrast, many fresh-faced and apparently open young executives have already hardened their hearts against anything not comprising 100 per cent self-interest.

To stop you jumping to the wrong conclusion, and to measure how important belief in your work is to you, we have devised The Personal Salvation Index. Answer the questions below quickly but as honestly as you can to find our how important corporate belief is to you. You must answer *yes* or *no* to each question – no fence-sitting is allowed – so if in doubt give the response that is closer to your view.

After you have taken the test, it may be apparent that some of your answers would change if you worked for a different organisation, one more worthy of your belief. If this is so, imagine that you were working for your 'dream' organisation, and take the test again. This will give a truer score for you.

More importantly, if there is significant difference in the two scores, find your ideal organisation!

The Personal Salvation Index

(You *must* answer *yes* or *no* to each question.)

Section A

1 If you won the pools, would you continue working?
2 Do you go home tired?
3 Do you often mention events at work to your family and friends?
4 Do you work more than 40 hours a week?
5 Do you work more than 50 hours a week?
6 Do you work more than 60 hours a week?
7 Do you like being asked at parties, 'What do you do?'
8 When asked 'What do you do?', do you reply in detail?
9 Do you get bored in the second week of a two-week holiday?
10 Do you sometimes dream about events at work?

Section B

11 Do you prefer to play singles rather than doubles at tennis?
12 Do you like walking alone?
13 Do you generally close the door of your office?
14 Do you like riding in an open-top car?
15 If forced to bet, would you back outsiders rather than favourites?
16 Do you tend to avoid gossip at work and get on with the job at hand?
17 Do you avoid having lunch with colleagues?
18 Do you prefer to keep your work and private lives largely separate?
19 Do you prefer to rush home after work rather than having a drink with workmates?
20 Do you try to avoid parties with lots of people you don't know?

Section C

21 Do you do voluntary work?
22 Do you belong to any sort of organised social club?
23 Do you prefer giving parties to going to other people's?
24 Are you sometimes unrealistic?
25 Do you believe in anything which you know is irrational?

26 Do you read horoscopes?

27 Do you go to church at least once a month?

28 Do you have a lucky number?

29 Do you believe there may be intelligent life on other planets?

30 Do you believe that people largely make their own success?

Section D

31 Are you a cynic?

32 Are you sometimes very critical of your organisation to people outside it?

33 Do you sometimes complain about life?

34 A prominent politician once said, 'There is no such thing as society', meaning that there were basically only individuals and families. Do you agree?

35 Do you believe in Original Sin (that most people are basically flawed)?

36 Have you learnt not to oppose the boss, even when you know he or she is wrong?

37 Have you ever played a practical joke on your workmates or one of them?

38 Are you basically a rebel (with or without a cause)?

39 Are you more of a hare than a tortoise?

40 Do you stick to your own area at work, rather than spend (or waste) time on the 'big picture'?

Section E

41 Do you sometimes get excited at work?

42 Do you enjoy praising your organisation?

43 Do you believe in progress?

44 If you had an excellent home and leisure life, and a well paid job at which you were good, would you care very much about what happened at work outside your immediate area?

45 Do you have a number of strong beliefs?

46 Do you like to understand what your colleagues are doing, even if it is largely irrelevant to doing your job well?

47 Do you give regularly to charity?

48 Do you think organisations should have an aim which everyone in the group understands and supports?

49 Do you read your organisation's newsletter carefully?

50 Do you sometimes waste time at work?

Section F

51 Do you spend a lot of time thinking how you can get promoted and/ or earn more money?

52 If you are honest, do you think you are basically superior to most other people in your organisation?

53 Is it more important to you to win yourself than to be part of a win- ning team?

54 Do you agree that your life outside work is much more important than your life at work?

55 Are you more of a realist than an optimist?

56 Do you agree that it is healthy to have a lot of people with fundamen- tally different values coexisting in the same organisation?

57 Do you agree that it is unrealistic to expect your leaders to spend most of their time being visible to the troops and communicating with them?

58 Are you fairly indifferent as to whether you understand the overall purpose of your organisation?

59 Do you generally let your head rule your heart?

60 Do you sometimes get embarrassed when people get emotionally com- mitted to their job?

Scoring your answers

- Score 1 point for each Yes answer in Section A.
- Score 1 point for each No answer in Section B.
- Score 1 point for each Yes answer in Section C.
- Score 1 point for each No answer in Section D.
- Score 2 points for each Yes answer in Section E.
- Score 4 points for each No answer in Section F.

Other answers (e.g. a No in Section A or a Yes in Section B) attract no points. Add up the total of points from all sections to derive your overall score.

Interpreting your score

The score you have could range from 0 to 100. No value judgement is attached to how highly you score, but the higher the score the greater the need for you to believe in your organisation.

0–20 You are an unwavering and consistent *heathen*, or, to be more polite, *atheist*. You could not care less which organisation you work for, as long as it gave you a good deal. There is no point in your becoming a leader.

21–45 You are firmly in the *unconverted* category. You could become a leader, but only in a totally different sort of organisation.

46–60 You're an *agnostic*. In some ways you would like to believe but you are very practical and pragmatic and tend to follow conventional wisdom. Think carefully what you do believe in, and what type of organisation you might like to lead.

61–80 *Hallelujah!* You're a *believer*. You want to work for an organisation with a purpose. You have clear leadership potential.

81–100 You believe – in your organisation, and in creating a better world. You may well become an influential leader.

Chapter 8

The Anatomy of Leadership

This chapter describes good leadership.

You can use the chapter to assess your current leadership, and also to assess your leadership skills.

1   Passion

The leaders must *care*. They must want to make the company something worth fighting for. They must be willing to invest part of themselves and a large chunk of their career in the company.

Are you readers willing to leave behind the security of the status quo? Ready for adversity, struggle, new standards and the demands of new ambitions? Could you see them lead a crusade?

Or are they 'career diplomats', serving their time, waiting for the next career move or retirement, or simply enjoying the perks of office and doing the minimum consistent with keeping them?

In making your judgement, do not confuse style and substance. Your leaders don't all have to be extroverts. Indeed, *none* of them need be. Some great leaders were notorious introverts. Clement Atlee, Britain's postwar Prime Minister, established the Welfare State despite communicating in short, cryptic, clipped sentences. Sir Owen Green, another introvert, established BTR as a great company with a clear mission. Both had few words but great passion (Atlee to eliminate poverty, Green to champion efficiency).

2   Determination

Passion is not enough. Determination to persevere despite setbacks is also essential. Many followed Moses over the Red Sea with high hopes but fell away during the long years in the wilderness. In contrast, Churchill and a few disciples in the late 1930s ploughed their lonely furrow, opposing Hitler and urging rearmament, steadfast in their determination.

No religion is ever established without setbacks, persecution or resistance. Included in the heading of *determination* are also *courage* and *street fighting instincts*. There will be factions within any organisation who will resist change.

The quest for progress may be dangerous and threaten an organisation's equilibrium. It may expose divisions within the group which have generally been ignored or papered over.

Powerful functions like Marketing or Production or Research may want to keep their operations a 'Black Box' or 'no-go area' to the rest of the company. A new religion may lead to awkward queries, inconvenient demands for higher output or standards, or, even worse, for interfunctional co-operation. Geographical territories may also resist the shrinking of the company's boundaries.

Unions may not like what is proposed, or see it as a way of weakening their hold over members.

And all this is just inside the organisation! The new religion may require a fresh approach to relationships with customers, suppliers, local communities and governments, and/or a new combativeness with competitors.

If courage is in short supply, it is better not to gird up for battle.

3   Honesty, integrity and values

Not just integrity. Open-mindedness and an ability to confront bad news are required too. The Board which views its group through rose-tinted spectacles will get no further to salvation than the cynical and time-serving Board.

Pride in an organisation is a fine thing to have, but if the leaders are defensive they will end up with a fairy-tale mission and toy-town results. The leaders must welcome objective criticism and search out the areas of improvement from their contacts with staff, customers and the outside world generally. A passion for excellence and the restless quest for improvement require dissatisfaction with the status quo and constant self-criticism.

The leadership must stand for certain values, and against certain values too. It must be clear that the leader thinks there is a right way to do things and expects others to follow his examples.

4   Vision

Not every corporate leader is a Moses, Martin Luther King or Chairman Mao. Leaders are not always visionaries. Visionaries are not usually chief executives.

But religion is all about vision. About how to make the future better. About how to soar above current difficulties and parochial concerns. About taking the flawed present and fashioning the potential future.

So somewhere within the top half-dozen or so people, or accessible to them, there must be a degree of vision. Half hidden, suppressed or latent: it doesn't matter so long as there is the germ of vision. It can be supplemented from visionary individuals further down the organisation.

5   Fit with the times

The leaders must have the right type of style and the right values for this stage of the organisation's existence. For example, if a firm has overexpanded due to overoptimistic sales forecasts, leading to a financial crisis, it might be totally appropriate to have an accountant promoted to chief executive, despite all his predecessors being from Marketing. On the other hand, it would probably not be a good fit to have an accountant lead a newly privatised utility whose main need is to become customer centred. The leader and the religion must fit the key challenges ahead.

6   A sense of the practical

The 'common touch' is useful, but what is essential is a nose for what will work and what will not, what can be made to stick and what is pious aspiration. All distinguished business leaders – as opposed to the whizz kids who are here today and bust tomorrow – have a sixth sense telling them what can be done in practice.

Religion is about aspiration, but the world is littered with false prophets who were long on vision and short on common sense. Do your leaders keep your feet on the ground even when their eyes are searching the heavens?

7   Time

Finally, the top team must be willing and able to set aside enough crusading time. This means that it must be *the* first call on time besides what is essential to run the business day to day. Operational fire fighting consumes an amount of time that those who have never been corporate chiefs cannot even begin to imagine. This leaves little enough time for all the important things, so if developing the religion is not the top priority, it simply will not happen.

This means that a top team facing the need to spend major amounts of time on other priorities – such as developing a new strategy or negotiating with regulators or integrating an acquisition or improving industrial relations – will not be able to develop a new religion as well. Remember that the total process will take three to five years, maybe more. If the leaders cannot allocate significant amounts of time for a sustained period, it is better not to start.

The *Leadership Checklist* can be used twice – once to assess your current leaders, and then to assess your own leadership potential.

The Leadership Checklist

1 Do you/your leaders care and have a passionate commitment to build a great organisation?
(a) Beyond question
(b) To some degree
(c) Not really

2 Are firmness of purpose and relentless determination hallmarks of you/your leaders?
(a) Yes
(b) To some degree
(c) You must be kidding

3 Do you/your leaders exude integrity, honesty and open mindedness?
(a) Yes
(b) To some degree
(c) Not much

4 Do you/your leaders have a clear vision and stand for clear values?
(a) Yes
(b) To some degree
(c) Not clearly

5 Do you/they fit the times?
(a) Yes
(b) To some degree
(c) No

6 Do you/your leader have a good nose for the practical?
(a) Yes
(b) Sometimes
(c) Not much

7 Do you/your leaders have both the time and inclination to lead a crusade?
(a) Yes
(b) Maybe
(c) No

Scoring

For Q1 score 40 points for (a), 15 for (b) or 0 for (c).
For Q2–7 score 10 points for each (a), 2 for each (b) and 0 for each (c).

Results for your leaders

80–100   There definitely is a leader in the house.
70–79   Leadership is probably just sufficient.
60–69   The top team should be sent on an outward bound course.
0–59   Send an emergency delegation to the headhunters.
Has your leadership passed the checklist test on the previous page?

Results for you

80–100   You are already a good leader or should become one.
70–79   You have leadership potential, but are probably trying to lead the wrong team.
60–69   Try the test again, but imagining you were leading your ideal group. If you score less than 80, forget about any leadership aspirations.
0–59   Concentrate on contributing to your team; do not try and lead it.

If your leaders are deficient, and you are a believer, you should either try to change the leadership or find another group or organisation to work in. This may not necessarily mean leaving your company, if you can find a role where the leadership is good or you can be the leader.

But what of your own leadership skills? If you scored less than 60, you are unlikely ever to be a good leader. Recognize this, and concentrate on being a good follower, under leaders you respect.

Yet if you scored at least 80, you really ought to find or create a leadership role somewhere. Good leaders don't grow on trees. Don't hang about – progress depends on people like you!

In becoming a leader, don't forget the lessons from the Moses Tour. These we now summarize and extend.

Chapter 9

Conclusion: Become a Leader!

The reasonable man adapts to the world. The unreasonable one persists in trying to adapt the world to himself. Therefore all progress depends on the unreasonable man.

George Bernard Shaw

Shaw was right. Progress depends on being dissatisfied with what we have, on wanting to build a better world. Mankind could have stayed in caves, because these were the only houses available. We could have stayed at the mercy of a cruel and indifferent Nature, fat and happy one season, and starving the next. Instead, we have built, mainly in the past two and a half centuries, a world of unprecedented wealth, a world of milk, honey, travel, leisure and pleasure for an almost unimaginable number of people.

Yet Shaw did not speak the whole truth. Progress depends not just on the unreasonable man and woman, but also on these people becoming leaders and exerting effective leadership. On her own, the unreasonable woman can achieve nothing – except being unreasonable. To change things, she has to find and inspire other people. She has to develop a blueprint for improvement, to persuade, to cajole, to commandeer resources, to organise them, to follow through. She has to form a group. And she has to inspire these people to inspire others to follow the new way. Thus the group expands. Progress snowballs. The new and better way becomes an epidemic. Thus she quite literally changes the world.

It follows that the most urgent and important task confronting human-kind is to expand the amount and quality of leadership at society's disposal.

Yet leadership is a fuzzy concept. There is no scientific measure of leadership, or understanding of how to manufacture it. Most peoples' ideas about leadership are naïve and unhelpful.

The Moses Tour gives us 11 invaluable lessons about leadership:

1   *Anyone can be a leader,* if they care enough about making a specific improvement.

2   *No-one can be a good leader without caring about something and being dissatisfied with the status quo.* The leader must have a Cause, an idea about something that needs changing.

3   *A leader needs followers.* To attract followers, you need not only a Cause, but also a group of people who will be attracted to the Cause, who will see personal benefit in supporting the Cause.

4   *A leader needs to time her bid for leadership.* The right time is when the Cause can attract sufficient support to break with the status quo.

5   *A leader and a Cause need an 'enemy',* something they are fighting against or getting away from.

6   *Leaders can only change things if they convert more and more people.* Leadership requires the new Cause – and later the new religion – to gain market share. Leaders must keep making new converts, and prevent existing converts from back-sliding. Leadership, like religion, works like a chain letter.

7   *Leaders don't have to have a fully fledged religion before they start.* You can start with a Cause. The religion evolves from the interaction of the tribe, the Cause, and the environment. All successful religions grow, develop and evolve to suit the needs of the time.

8   *Leaders need to lead by actions. Actions lead to imitation.* Words are much less effective. Leaders need to be visible, to be observed. Leaders go among their people. When leaders became remote, they cannot lead.

9   *Leaders must enforce discipline and impose new behaviour standards.* Without new and improved standards, the religion will not impress. Behaviour

cannot be controlled without well-defined values and standards. Once the religion has been defined, those who do not meet the standards must be exposed. *A new religion must be intolerant of those who do not subscribe to it.*

10   *When the leaders have achieved what they set out to achieve, they should go.* New leaders should take over who can evolve the religion to suit new circumstances. Without evolution, the religion will ossify and start to decline.

11   *The most effective way to start a new religion is to spin off from an existing religion.* The Cause can be born within the womb of the old organisation. The break, when it comes, is effective, because only a few committed people break away to start afresh.

★★★

The world will never have too many good leaders. The requirements are exacting. Even good leaders may fail, because they choose the wrong task, the wrong people, or the wrong time. Changing the world is not easy.

Many people imagine that leadership is correlated with hierarchy, and that democracy and decentralisation require less leadership. They have it exactly wrong. A democratic and decentralised society is one that operates by market rules and requires initiative from all citizens. This type of society will always have a severe deficit of leadership.

Progress requires people to exercise their initiative, to say, 'we could do this better'. A decentralised society allows people to say such things and to act on them. It allows new groups to spring up, new small companies to be formed, new voluntary groups to right wrongs, new ways of doing things to be tried by existing organisations. None of these things can happen without leadership. In an ideal society, we will all be leaders, and we will all be followers. There are so many spheres of life that can be improved that there is room for every single person to be a leader in something.

Become a leader. Look for your Cause – at work, at home, in politics, anywhere. Look for some followers. Get them across the Red Sea and you are away. You will be inspired by the journey.

And when you've succeeded in one sphere of leadership, leave it alone. Find another sphere where leadership is required. Keep repeating the process.

Progress depends on your leadership. Now, tomorrow, and as long as you live.

Appendices for Business Leaders

Introduction

I have written this book for leaders and aspiring leaders of all types, not just business folk. But I have a particular interest in business leadership, because it is so leveraged. The progress of society in the past 250 years has been driven pre-eminently by business progress working through companies (large and small) and markets. We are still at the foothills of this progress.

One reason for optimism is that current business structures and ways of working are severely sub-optimal. They could be much better than they are. If they were, tremendous and perhaps unimaginable amounts of wealth could be liberated, while simultaneously working lives would be transformed, mainly for the better.

Business practices and structures are generally very primitive. Most corporations are too large, and nearly all of them are too complex. One may question whether the dominant type of large company today, the multibusiness corporation, will be so dominant – or even typical – in the future. This is a large subject which is covered in three recent books.* But the most important reason why our existing corporations are pale reflections of what they should (and probably will) become is that they are administratively- and process-driven rather than leadership- and purpose-driven.

The three Appendices that follow explain the difference between the administrative/process-driven corporation and the leadership/purpose-driven corporation. Appendix A asks, 'Is Your Company Damned?' It allows you to diagnose what type of corporation yours is, and whether it is beyond redemption. Appendix B outlines the mountain that must be climbed to turn managers into leaders. This is no trivial task, either for an individual corporation or for business as a whole: leadership is necessary, but management is entrenched behind its sandbags, and it will take a revolution to replace management with leadership. Finally, Appendix C explains 'Why firms with religion will win' – the competitive advantage that 'religious' firms, driven by purpose, increasingly enjoy.

---

* see David Sadtler, Andrew Campbell and Richard Koch (1997) *Breakup! When Large Companies Are Worth More Dead Than Alive*, Oxford, Capstone/New York, The Free Press; Richard Koch (1996, 1997) *Managing Without Management*, London/Sonoma, CA, Nicholas Brealey; and Richard Koch (1997, 1998) *The 80/20 Principle*, London, Nicholas Brealey/New York, Doubleday Currency.

Is Your Company Damned?

Redemption is a central tenet of most religions. Salvation is available, provided certain conditions are met. The conditions may be onerous, but faith and a willingness to cast oneself upon the mercy of God mean that redemption is available for all. The individual sinner is grist to the salvation mill, regardless of past sins. For religions, the more saved the better, and the worse the sinner, the better the salvation.

Alas, when it comes to companies, it is not realistic to take such a charitable view. The past has a way of ruling out certain futures. If a company is damned, it may be better to give up – to leave, or sell the company – than to struggle pushing water up-hill.

Barriers on the road to redemption

Some companies are pretty much beyond the pale. Companies are not blank cheques on which a person can write his or her own demands, even as the chief executive. Every firm has its own culture and history. This heritage may be good or bad, but it should never be ignored: if it is, it will take revenge.

Equally, every company has a power structure and there is always a power of veto, which may rest in the hands of one person, a small number of people or sometimes a very large group.

And finally, all firms operate in a market and competitive context of some sort, and may or may not have worked out a sensible strategy to survive and prosper in the coming years.

So when it comes to working out a common purpose or sense of mission for a company, we should be aware of three potential pitfalls, any of which may prove fatal.

Pitfall 1: history and culture

No company can successfully develop a crusade that contradicts its history and culture, unless a revolution in strategy and politics has just occurred.

Pitfall 2: politics

No company can successfully develop a crusade if its top management is divided and/or not totally committed to the process.

Pitfall 3: strategy

No company can successfully develop a crusade unless it already has a sensible business strategy that will work.

If your company suffers from any of these pitfalls, it will be a waste of time (and a diversion of much needed effort) to try to develop a sense of common purpose. Sort out the underlying issues first (if this is possible) and only then come back to the question of your company's purpose. Let's now examine each of these hurdles.

History and culture

One of the strengths of a new boss is that he or she can bring a fresh approach uncluttered by the baggage of history and a company's dearly held myths. But we should also remember Warren Buffet's caution that 'when a company with a reputation for failure is taken over by a management with a reputation for success, it is usually the company's reputation that survives intact.'

This is not just a matter of success or failure. It's a matter of taste and inclination too. It may be economically logical to take a company in a particular direction. But, if it offends against a company's deeply rooted beliefs or culture, it just won't work. Mars scored an amazing success by moving from its base chocolate confectionery market into a new segment of the ice-cream market, which it created: ice-cream confectionery. Given the relative weakness of the main ice-cream companies in terms of product development and brand name, it might make perfect economic success for Mars to build on its invasion by deciding to dominate the wider ice-cream market. In fact, to defend the ice-cream confectionery segment, it may be strategically necessary to broaden out. The only sensible action would be to buy one of the existing ice-cream companies and combine operations to create a broad line supplier.

Let's imagine for the sake of argument that one of these companies is available and that the economic case is very favourable, but the only way even Mars could afford the ice-cream company would be to take on a significant burden of debt.

Would it be sensible for Mars to have as part of its mission a decision to develop and dominate the ice-cream market by the year 2000, in the same way it has become a world leader in chocolate confectionery? On the face of it, yes. But that would be to ignore the Mars culture, which jealously protects its independence and refuses to take on any serious amount of debt because it doesn't want outsiders to have too much influence. Even if a new chief executive wanted to lead the company this way, it would be putting at risk a central aspect of Mars' purpose – its independence.

Of course, sometimes a company has to change its direction and culture. In the early 1980s Firestone had to stop making tyres and turn itself into a service organisation. About the same time Gestetner had to move from a production culture, get out of making photocopiers and concentrate on service too. But successful moves such as these are nearly always the result of crisis, poor financial results and an internal revolution. In both Firestone and Gestetner a new strategy was developed, new management installed and a conscious effort made to change the culture. People knew that there was a major change, a discontinuity, in the way they should behave and in the company's direction.

It comes down to this: a totally new mission can only come after a revolution in a company's strategy, politics and culture. It can follow this revolution pretty quickly, so much so it appears to be part of the same revolution. But you cannot start by sitting down to work out a revolutionary new mission, and then use this as the basis for change, because the new mission will have no roots and no power. A new mission which goes against the grain of the firm's culture and history simply will not stick.

Politics

Quite often a company decides, usually as part of a major strategic review, to adopt a 'mission statement'. Typically the head of corporate planning persuades the chief executive that the strategy would be incomplete without a mission. The corporate planning director involves a few colleagues, he may even talk to outside experts and buy a few books on mission, and then he prepares his draft mission. Sometimes he hires outside consultants to help or involves the company's communications people, who are dab hands at crafting fine-sounding copy. He then discusses this with the chief executive and the Board, who tinker around with it and then agree they like it.

The mission statement is then officially promulgated and copies start appearing on notice boards, in the newsletter and in the annual report. New recruits are given a copy and told how important it is.

And absolutely nothing else happens that is different from what went before. There is not a whit more sense of purpose or common direction than there was before the exercise.

Why hasn't it worked?

Simply because those who run the company have not passionately wanted to develop a purpose for it.

It isn't really their mission. Sure, they approved it. Certainly, they were involved in the process, *but they didn't make it happen.* They didn't sweat blood over it or give birth to it. They didn't demand it. It was suggested to them and they went along with it. It was handed to them on a plate.

Unless those who run the company really want to create a sense of common purpose, any such exercise is dead in the water before it starts.

But even assume that *one* of the top people – perhaps the chairman or the chief executive – wants to define a mission and is terribly keen on it. It still won't work unless *all* the people who run the company are or become equally committed.

The wily leader will therefore very often decide to wait before a powerful baron retires from the board – or self-destructs – before attempting to develop a mission, because the leader knows that the baron would prove obstructive and destroy for ever the chance the leader has to found his religion. It may be necessary to wait for years.

A naïve attempt to get consensus from a top management with different religious inclinations can cause explosions. The would-be messiah can end up getting crucified.

Often there is no consensus between the top people on a company's direction. For example, in one pharmaceutical company the R&D director insisted that all the company's success was because it was 'R&D driven' and that all the company's values were tied up with innovative research. The chief executive and the marketing director, on the other hand, felt that the company had to get into the top world league of pharmaceutical companies, and that the keynotes for the company should be growth and personal opportunity. This sounded fine, but the rub was that R&D would have to commit to a definite and faster timetable for new drug development. The finance director (surprisingly) then argued that this would kill the company, as it would cramp the individuality of the scientists.

Both sides of the argument were plausible, but the issues were not confronted and dealt with. A compromise statement was reached, which all parties believed reflected their own point of view. It is too early to know whether the new mission will prove useful. But it's odds on that the marketing director and research director are continuing to promote their opposing interests.

When we say that all of those who run the company must be passionate believers in the new corporate purpose, it is important to be realistic. There is a real difficulty in having this happen if a company has a 'democratic' and large top management, and especially if it has a matrix organisation or is run by committee. It is difficult to see Shell, for example, ever developing what we would consider a proper sense of corporate purpose. Shell is in many ways a fine and successful company, but it is also a vast sprawling bureaucracy where power is distributed in a large number of nooks and crannies, some in London, some in the Hague, and some stashed away in the important operating centres around the globe. Shell's strength lies in its professionalism, not its passion.

For most companies the task is not so daunting. In the US it is literally true that most companies, including some very large ones, are run by one person, the Chief Executive Officer. There is needs only one person passionately to want a corporate purpose, and it becomes possible. In the UK, the idea of one person running any major company has gone out of fashion since the fall of Ernest Saunders, Asil Nadir and Robert Maxwell, though there is still a minority of big companies where it is still true. More usually, British companies are run by two to five people, who, if they are agreed on a course of action, can push it through effectively. In these cases it is the two to five people who must really want and agree on the corporate purpose, which can then be endorsed by Boards and all the other formal mechanisms. On the Continent there is a wide variety of practice, but most companies are run by fewer than ten people.

It follows, then, that to define a company's purpose first requires defining who runs the company. Unless the people who run the company want a purpose and feel passionately about the company, no progress can be made.

Sometimes, therefore, the wish to examine corporate purpose or mission leads back to the more basic question of power in an organisation. In many cases it is impossible to change the attitudes and values of top managers. Unity cannot be achieved with the existing power group. The choice then becomes: either to abandon the quest for corporate purpose, or to decide to change some of the top management before starting the process. In our experience it is not at all unusual for corporate purpose initiatives to lie dormant until certain individuals leave the group. This may seem ruthless but it is far better than indecision and mediocrity.

Strategy

When you are 21, it is all bright, confident morning. You believe that most things are possible: that you can achieve pretty much what you want in any field of endeavour. By the age of 40, sadly, even the most successful people are much more modest and realistic about their areas of expertise and focus.

It's the same for companies. An imaginative young person might be able to think of all sorts of creative and appealing futures for a company, but only some of them would be economically realistic or fit with the focus that the company has. We might want Rover to become world leader in mass-market cars. But Ford and General Motors stand in the way, as do the Japanese, German, French and Italian competitors. A mission built around this goal would be pointless.

A good mission for a company is built on a sensible commercial strategy. If there is doubt about the strategy, or if there is more than one sensible strategy, or if different strategies would imply radically different types of company in the future, it makes sense to develop the new strategy and the mission in tandem with each other. The process may take longer. But it is better to get it right than to work against the grain of economic reality.

In the spirit of Chapters 1 and 2 we have devised a further test – a test of whether your company is ready for redemption. Ken Miki, the leading mission consultant in Japan, tells us that before he takes on a client he asks the client to commission 'a readiness audit'. A team from Miki's organisation spends up to six months understanding the client with the purpose of determining whether the company is ready to review its purpose and philosophy. Usually this results in finding that the client is not yet ready. As Miki explains, it may then be some years before he does work with the company: before he judges that the company is ready for a deep examination of its purpose and philosophy.

I cannot assess the readiness of your company with the thoroughness of Ken Miki. So I've developed the Redemption Readiness test. By scoring the following questions, you can judge whether a review of purpose, philosophy and mission is worth embarking on.

The test below enables you to decide whether it is timely or too early to save your company. Administer the test to a sample of colleagues and compare results to be sure of the answer.

Is your company damned?

1 How many people are there who really run your company (i.e. who have to give their approval to any major decision)?
(a) One
(b) Between two and five
(c) Six to ten
(d) Over ten.

2 Are those who run the company pretty much agreed on what its strategy and values should be?
(a) Yes
(b) Largely
(c) To some degree, but there are some important differences of opinion
(d) There are major disagreements, but some common consensus values
(e) There are at least two major camps which have basically different strategies and values.

3 When there are differences of opinion on important issues, what happens?
(a) The most powerful person (in each area of decision making) goes ahead regardless of opposition
(b) Issues are confronted, there is a fight, but a decision is made which everyone then sticks to
(c) There is a fight and a decision is made, but the losers try to undermine the course decided upon
(d) A compromise is reached which everyone can live with
(e) There is a discussion until everyone is convinced the right decision has been made.

4 Do those who run the company really, deeply, want it to have a clear purpose or mission?
(a) Yes
(b) Yes, but they realise that the top group is not sufficiently united to do this yet
(c) Some do and some don't
(d) Most don't, one or two do
(e) No one does.

5 Is the organisation too busy struggling for survival or in the midst of an upheaval, so that there is not time to think about anything else right now?
(a) Yes
(b) No.

6 How good are the organisation's top people at leadership?
(a) They combine the charisma of Moses, John F. Kennedy, Malcolm X and Martin Luther King
(b) They're pretty effective, in their own ways
(c) They need help and support to effect change, but are capable of leading quite well when they realise the need for it
(d) They have all had charisma by-pass operations, and would not recognise leadership if it hit them
(e) Frankly, they're not very good, but not totally hopeless either.

7 Is there a power struggle at the top which needs to be resolved?
(a) Yes
(b) No
(c) Possibly/I'm not sure.

8 How well supported by facts and a clear consensus within the organisation is its commercial strategy?
(a) Very well: the strategy is clear, commands overwhelming support inside the organisation, and is working well
(b) It's pretty well supported by facts and consensus in most important areas
(c) Some major issues need to be decided and it isn't clear which way to go
(d) Not at all.

9 Is the organisation in financial crisis?
(a) Yes
(b) To some degree, there are some serious problems
(c) Not really, though there are some concerns
(d) No, there are no financial pressures at all.

10 Is the organisation undergoing a turbulent period of management change?
(a) Yes
(b) Not yet, but it's coming soon
(c) No.

11 Is the organisation experiencing a 'cultural revolution?'
(a) Yes, definitely
(b) To some degree
(c) No.

Scoring your answers

1 Score 10 for (a), 0 for (b), 15 for (c), or 25 for (d).
2 Score 0 for (a), 2 for (b), 7 for (c), 12 for (d), or 25 for (e).
3 Score 10 for (a), 2 for (b), 20 for (c), 16 for (d), or 0 for (e).
4 Score 0 for (a), 5 for (b), 20 for (c), 23 for (d), or 25 for (e).
5 Score 20 for (a), or 0 for (b).
6 Score 0 for (a), 2 for (b), 4 for (c), 20 for (d), or 16 for (e).
7 Score 20 for (a), 0 for (b), or 8 for (c).
8 Score 0 for (a), 2 for (b), 16 for (c), or 20 for (d).
9 Score 10 for (a), 3 for (b), 0 for (c), or 10 for (d).
10 Score 5 for (a), 10 for (b), or 0 for (c).
11 Score 5 for (a), 3 for (b), or 0 for (c).

Interpreting your scores

The scores measure the current difficulty in 'redeeming' your organisation, with a higher score meaning greater difficulty:

0 to 30   *The company is definitely ready for 'redemption'.*

31 to 55   *The company is not quite ready:* one or two vital pre-conditions need to be met, but you are not far off. Take the test again once there has been significant change on these dimensions (such as a shake up in the boardroom).

55 to 75   *It's too early to save the company:* a lot of change is required before you can contemplate developing a purpose that will stick. Take the test again later, but only after there has been a serious upheaval.

Over 75   *Your company may be beyond redemption:* so few conditions for developing a sensible purpose exist that you should definitely not attempt to develop a corporate purpose in the near or medium term. On the other hand, nothing is for ever, and if your organisation undergoes a revolution of earth shattering proportions, take the test again then.

What does 'beyond redemption' mean?

If you work in a company categorised as *beyond redemption*, this does not mean that it is about to go bust. It just means that it is unlikely to be able to develop a really satisfying sense of common mission. You then have to decide whether to continue in a company without a soul or to jump ship when the conditions are right.

Frankly, the more mobile should move. It's much more fun working for a company which has *'it'* than one which doesn't.

If it's *too early to save* your organisation you may be in a position to accelerate the process. If you are a top manager, don't delay.

Ready for treatment

Let's assume that your company is neither beyond redemption nor waiting for some preconditions to be met. The key issue now is not whether the company is ready, but whether top management will do anything about it.

If not, and if you are a middle manager, lobby your bosses. Considering that most companies do not have *'it'*, it's remarkably easy to get colleagues or bosses to agree that *'it'* is a good thing to have. And if managers are calling for definition of a company's mission, it is difficult for any chief executive to turn a deaf ear. In British Airways, Colin Marshall resisted the advice of his personnel function, believing that the company was not ready for a public examination of its strategy, values and philosophy. But the pressure he received from managers as a result of speaking to the frequent 'Managing People First' programmes convinced him that his managers were ready, even if the power group at the top was still working out differences.

So go ahead: demand *'it'*. Let your leaders know that you feel there is something lacking. Explain your sense of emptiness. It's not like asking for a pay rise: a sense of purpose benefits everyone and has no financial cost.

But can you turn managers into leaders? We will see next how difficult this can be.

Appendix B

Converting Managers into Leaders: the Challenge Below-Decks

The management scourge

Every large corporation contains thousands, tens of thousands, sometimes even hundreds of thousands, of 'managers'. A large proportion of these, in some corporations even a majority, are there for one reason only: to manage the corporation's internal processes. As Geoff Mulgan has observed, '... anyone who has worked in a large bureaucracy knows most of its energy is used simply reproducing itself. The same is true for the classic modern corporation.' Many managers subtract more value from customers and owners than they add.

The test of whether someone is a 'manager' in this bad sense is very simple. The acid test is whether a majority of her time is spent on activities that clearly add value to customers, directly or indirectly. A remarkable number of managers fail this simple test. Their jobs should be abolished. Despite the hoo-hah occasioned by downsizing and re-engineering, corporations are still stuffed with managers who add little value to customers, many of them actually being of negative value.

Managerial trade-unionism

Management is of much greater sociological than economic significance. Now that, in most places, trade unions have been tamed, management is the last great interest group exercising collective power greater than its economic contribution. In many large corporations, managers are unaccountable. Their corporations compete largely against other large corporations, similarly choc-a-bloc with excessive management. Investors do not know and cannot punish the management over-manning. The only sanction of the market, one that is working but with little evident deterrent effect, is that small corporations are at last starting to gain market share against large corporations, despite all the latters' inherent advantages. If managers continue to behave as a class, and continue to create unnecessary jobs for each other, the abolition of surplus management will continue to be an extremely slow process.

Antidotes to management

There are only two antidotes to surplus management: entrepreneurship and leadership.

Entrepreneurs nibble from without – they eat the managers' lunch, or, to be more precise, the managers' shareholders' lunch.

The only antidote to surplus management that can operate from within is leadership.

Leadership is inherently anti-management. Management is a process, a routine, an established way of doing things: a conservative set of relationships, interested above all in managerial self-preservation. Leadership, in contrast, is interested in results and obsessed with changing things. Leadership does not neglect self-interest, but it seeks self-interest through other-interest, through changing the world – and in business, this means principally the world of the customer – for the better. Leadership seeks progress. Leadership looks at customer value. Leadership overturns vested interests. It should be clear that leadership and management are set for a train smash.

Top leaders are bloody revolutionaries

Leaders like Jack Welch of GE, Percy Barnevik of ABB, Bill Weiss of Ameritech, Ted Turner of CNN, Richard Branson of Virgin, or Bill Gates of Microsoft are not interested in preserving management's processes or perquisites. They want results. They want advances in customer service and in new generations of product for customers. They are revolutionaries. Like revolutionaries, they are iconoclasts, they wish to smash the past and recreate the future. Like revolutionaries, they go for the jugular. Like revolutionaries, they create blood on the floor. Like revolutionaries, they want a new heaven and a new earth. Like revolutionaries, they create a new sense of purpose. Like revolutionaries, they use blatant and lurid propaganda. Like revolutionaries, they are restless and unpredictable. Like revolutionaries, they use the language of democracy and the weapons of dictators. Like revolutionaries, they take on the establishment. Like revolutionaries, they simplify, divide, unite and transform. Like revolutionaries, they are hard acts to live with and hard acts to follow. Like revolutionaries, they are the mainspring of progress and the hope of mankind.

It is much more difficult to be a low-level leader

Yet, the top level of level of leadership is, comparatively, the easy part. It is easier to be a revolutionary in the executive suite than in the canteen manager's office or that of the office services manager. The top revolutionaries may swoop and dive, chop and restructure, opine and disappear, materialising and dematerialising at will across the corporate canvas. For the canteen manager to become a revolutionary is much rarer, and more difficult, than for the CEO. She, the canteen manager, may have to abolish her own role and outsource the feeding, to add the most value. If she is lucky, 'all' she may have to do to convert from a manager to a leader may be to overturn all her established practices and ways of thinking, and the habits of a lifetime. It is asking a lot. The grain of corporate structure and corporate practice is deeply resistant to revolution and to leadership. Human decency, as well as self-interest, recoils from destroying managerial structures.

Micro-leadership: the real breakthrough

This is why, if large corporations are to become de-magnified, to swap their management impregnation for leadership impregnation, it is vital for each level of management to be allowed to create its own sub-religion, its own leadership, within a broad church of the new corporate religion. The canteen supervisor must come up with her own road to progress, her own Cause, her own route across the Red Sea, and ultimately her own religion. Her gospel of progress may be healthier food, it may be greater value, it may be to turn the canteens into a place where customers can meet their corporate servants, it may be anything she likes – as long as the Cause appeals to her co-workers and contributes, ultimately, in a small or large way, to a more responsive and customer-centred corporation.

If leadership is ever to replace management in large corporations, there must be very many leaders and very many religions. When it comes to leadership, small may be beautiful. Whizz-bang leadership at the top, the fireworks of the charismatic CEO, are all very well. Only when the poor bloody infantry down below convert from being managers to being leaders, their own leaders, will large corporations stand a chance of reversing their slow and insensible decay at the hands of a thousand smaller rivals.

Why Firms with Religion Will Win

This is where (perhaps to your relief) we leave the *Old Testament* analogy. We also set aside all the trappings of so-called management science, where despite a general lack of intellectual rigour there is some quite convincing evidence that organisations that liberate their employees' abilities perform better financially.

Organisations that have a strong sense of purpose – 'religion' – will win over those that do not. Organisations with purpose are in a minority today. They will be in a majority in the future. Today's dominant type of administratively and process driven corporation will become a dinosaur. The future belongs to the purpose driven corporation, the 'religious' corporation.

Most employees – and especially the talented and ambitious ones – would rather work in a purpose-driven corporation than in the typical process-driven corporation.

Most companies do not provide this sense of common purpose. Some do. Some never will.

Those individuals who want to have a meaningful purpose should join a company that can provide one. In the past, people have not sought out companies with a sense of purpose. But awareness is growing. In the future, they will.

So purpose driven companies will be able to draw on a wider and more discriminating pool of potential employees, who are likely to be both able (because they are mobile) and highly dedicated when in the right firm.

Two key social trends

Something else is happening in society. There are two changes: one in the way firms should be run internally, for maximum effectiveness; and the other in the way that the market selects winners.

Change one: farewell to the jackboot

Internally, it is becoming both difficult and inefficient to run firms based on command, instruction and close supervision. Wealth creation requires initiative of a highly flexible nature. Even in relatively humble jobs, like production worker or shop assistant, knowledge, initiative and a positive attitude are increasingly necessary, as technology, customised product/service provision and responsiveness to customers all become more important.

Decisions have to be made without being able to refer the matter to the supervisor or the boss, and without a thick instruction manual.

These decisions can only be made effectively if the culture of a firm and its policy guidelines are well known, internalised by each member of the firm, and consistently held between different people and functions within the firm.

This requires a sense of common purpose within a framework of shared values.

Change two: competing for people

The second, and related, change in society is that companies are coming to compete as much or more for their *people* as for their *markets* or *raw materials*.

What for example is the competitive advantage of Marks & Spencer as against British Home Stores, a much less successful chain store with the same type of products? They have the same type of premises in the same types of places. They have access to the same suppliers of goods, and to the same information technology. They should be able to attract the same type of customer, because they are both broadly mass-market retailers.

Marks & Spencer's advantage is in its people and its culture, and in the brand that embodies these attributes.

Increasingly, developed countries have economies based on knowledge, service and technology rather than low cost production. Knowledge, service and technology rely upon the people power of the firm.

Two terrific advantages for purpose-driven firms

Firms with purpose have two advantages here. First, they can attract and retain the best people, because more people want to work for them, so they can afford to be more choosy.

Second, firms with purpose make more of the collective people power they have at their disposal, because time is not wasted on duplication of effort or unproductive conflict (though there is still and should be quite a lot of constructive conflict), and because people simply work harder, longer and more intelligently.

So firms with purpose will gain market share and be more profitable than those without purpose. Because they compete more effectively for people, firms with purpose will end up winning customers too.

The future is coming faster

The rise of 'purpose' winners has been slow because we have had the wrong model of success. In the East, purpose power is recognised. In the West it is a newer phenomenon.

In the West, we have focused on outputs rather than inputs. On profit rather than what produces it. We have had the wrong time horizon, and a hopelessly anachronistic ideology of management priorities based on the nineteenth-century joint stock company.

We have sought to extract value rather than create it. We have been ruled by accountants, and bled off our leaders into social and artistic avenues. We have forgotten that our great industrial founders had *ideas* for their firms, and a vision of something they wanted to create. They rarely fretted about their stock market value or sought an 'exit' as soon as they could sell the firm.

The management philosophy of much of the post-World War II era in the West, and especially the 1980s, was little more than 'Smash, Grab & Run'. Few talked about building for the twenty-first century.

And, for a time, the 'irreligious' West lost ground to the purposeful firms from the East.

Now, all this is beginning to change. Purpose is becoming respectable. Leaders are beginning to emerge, to refound great companies which have lost their way, and to start new ones. The working individual is coming into his and her own, no longer content to leave their souls at home or rely upon consumption to give meaning to life.

It cannot happen soon enough. You can make it happen. You can speed it up. You have nothing to lose but your consumer chains. The world has nothing to lose but discredited dogma, accountants, stockbrokers and management consultants. There is a whole universe to gain: a universe of meaningful work, human dignity, service to the community, and greater prosperity too.

Demand that your company acquires a real purpose, its own religion. If it fails to do so, take your body, brain and soul elsewhere. If enough of us start doing this, the transformation in our personal and collective fortunes will be sudden and startling.

Short Bibliography

The subject of leadership has spawned a huge library. Rather than provide a guide to conventional wisdom, here are a few books that follow up on this book's themes. This is, therefore, a list for those who enjoyed the book rather than for those who are seeking something better.

1   Charles Farkas, Philippe De Backer and Allen Sheppard (1995) *Maximum Leadership*, London, Orion. A spirited attempt to categorize different types of leadership.

2   Max De Pree (1989) *Leadership is an Art*, Michigan/London, Michigan State University Press/Arrow Business Books. Balanced and instructive.

3   James O'Toole (1995) *Leading Change*, San Francisco, Jossey-Bass. A radical and humanist approach from a stimulating thinker, Vice-President of The Aspen Institute.

4   Tom Peters (1988) *Thriving on Chaos: Handbook for a Management Revolution*, New York, Knopf/London, Macmillan. The first Peters attack on conventional management.

5   Tom Peters (1992) *Liberation Management*, New York, Knopf. A goldmine of leadership vignettes sprouting from uncontrolled and often incoherent prose.

6   Meredith Belbin (1984) *Management Teams: Why they succeed or fail*, Oxford, Butterworth Heinemann. The classic text on team working, identifying different roles. Belbin's approach is technocratic and in-

strumental; he is not much interested in what the team try to do. But leaders working with teams will find much of interest here.

7 Warren Bennis and Burt Nanus (1985) *Leaders: The Strategies for Taking Charge*, New York, Harper & Row. A study of 90 leaders from many walks of life. Bennis and Nanus first contrasted leadership with bureaucracy. They insist, eloquently, that leadership can be taught.

8 James MacGregor Burns (1978) *Leadership*, New York, Harper & Row. A brilliant and enduring book from a political scientist that stresses the need for leaders 'to arouse, engage and satisfy the motives of followers.' He also stresses the moral attributes of leadership: 'moral leadership emerges from, and always returns to, the fundamental wants and needs, aspirations and values of the followers.'

9 Richard Koch and Ian Godden (1996) *Managing Without Management*, London, Nicholas Brealey. A controversial attack on management and a plea for business simplicity, entrepreneurship and leadership in large corporations.

10 David Sadtler, Andrew Campbell and Richard Koch (1997) *Breakup! When Large Corporations are Worth More Dead Than Alive*, Oxford, Capstone. A careful examination of the trend towards breaking up large corporations via spin-offs and demergers. Contains a circumspect but menacing attack on head offices and a plea for smaller and simpler corporations.

11 Richard Koch (1994) *The New Boss's First 100 Days*, London, Pitman. A populist and straight-talking guide for new bosses at every level. Looks at what leadership means down in the trenches.

Acknowledgements

Beyond Moses and the anonymous chroniclers of his epic journey, this book owes the greatest debt to Andrew Campbell, co-founder of the Ashridge Strategic Management Centre. When Andrew was already a distinguished author and academic, and I was neither (whether distinguished or otherwise!), Andrew agreed to co-write my first book, *Wake Up and Shake Up your Company* (Financial Times Pitman, 1993). Some of the material in *Moses on Leadership* is adapted from the earlier book and therefore owes a substantial debt to Andrew.

Moreover, Andrew has helped me in writing this book by contributing ideas, insights, critiques and his own brand of intellectual stimulation. Many of the most powerful ideas here are his, though I'm sure he would agree that all of the mistakes are mine.

My partners-in-crime at Capstone, Richard Burton and Mark Allin, were also responsible for leading me to revisit the Moses story. No-one could wish for more friendly and intelligent collaborators.

Most of this book was written in South Africa and I am very grateful for the hospitality extended to me in this most beautiful of countries by so many friends, especially Dr Chris Eyles, Elizabeth and David Miller and Vicky Carlton. Special thanks also to Antony Ball and Thierry Dalais.

And, finally, thanks to Lee.

Index